Just Love Her

Just Love Her

Thoughts on How to Not Just Live in but Glorify God
in the Middle of My "Bad" Marriage

↭

D. E. Fast

FOREWORD BY
G. Michael Wortham

RESOURCE *Publications* • Eugene, Oregon

JUST LOVE HER
Thoughts on How to Not Just Live in but Glorify God in the Middle of My "Bad" Marriage

Copyright © 2022 D. E. Fast. All rights reserved. Except for brief quotations in critical publications or reviews, no part of this book may be reproduced in any manner without prior written permission from the publisher. Write: Permissions, Wipf and Stock Publishers, 199 W. 8th Ave., Suite 3, Eugene, OR 97401.

Resource Publications
An Imprint of Wipf and Stock Publishers
199 W. 8th Ave., Suite 3
Eugene, OR 97401

www.wipfandstock.com

PAPERBACK ISBN: 978-1-6667-3744-8
HARDCOVER ISBN: 978-1-6667-9689-6
EBOOK ISBN: 978-1-6667-9690-2

Scripture quotations marked (NLT) are taken from the Holy Bible, New Living Translation, copyright ©1996, 2004, 2015 by Tyndale House Foundation. Used by permission of Tyndale House Publishers, Carol Stream, Illinois 60188. All rights reserved.

Scripture quotations taken from the (NASB®) New American Standard Bible®, copyright © 1960, 1971, 1977, 1995, 2020 by The Lockman Foundation. Used by permission. All rights reserved.

Scripture quotations taken from the Amplified® Bible (AMPC), copyright © 1954, 1958, 1962, 1964, 1965, 1987 by The Lockman Foundation. Used by permission.

Scripture quotations marked MSG are taken from THE MESSAGE, copyright © 1993, 2002, 2018 by Eugene H. Peterson. Used by permission of NavPress, represented by Tyndale House Publishers. All rights reserved.

Any references to historical events, real people, or real places are used fictitiously. Names, characters, and places are products of the author's imagination.

Dedication

This book is dedicated to wife, Laurie. Other than God, you are the glue that holds our family together. You are the ultimate Proverbs 31 woman and the best mom ever! Thank you for loving me. I love you, Laurie.

Table of Contents

Foreword xi
Preface xiii

Why Write This? 3
To Whom?
You Won't Be Able to Do This 7
Motivational Verses 9
Helpful Books to Consider Reading 12
A Little Background 14
This Is Not One of Those Books 17
The Relational Iceberg 20
"Bad" Marriages 22
The *Whys* of My "Bad" Marriage 26
"Bad" Wife Identifiers 29
Grace? 32
Accepting the "Bad" with the Good 34
Offended by My "Bad" Marriage? 41
Did God Really Put Us Together? 47
Everybody Plays Broken 51
An Imperfect Marriage Is Perfectly OK 55
If He Were My Number One Passion, She Wouldn't Be My Number One Problem 60
Love Him, When You "Can't" Love Her 65
Turbocharging the Love-Him-When-You-"Can't"-Love-Her Thing 68
Placing the Truth of God over Emotions 71

Table of Contents

Dipping Toes and Letting Goes 75
With a Significant *Why*, We (He and I) Can Handle Any *What* 78
What's Impossible for Me Is a Walk in the Park for Him 83
Which Is a Bigger Deal, That You Get Satisfied or That God Gets Glorified? 87
Which Is More Important to You? 91
Sacrifice It 94
Suffering 97
Suffering II 100
Pain 102
Pain II 105
Pain III 108
Pain IV 111
I Choose to Suffer Because... 113
Forgiveness 117
Forgiveness II 122
Resentments 127
Resentments II 131
Placing Intellect over Emotion 138
"I Choose Us" 143
You Are My Life; She Is My Wife 145
A Full Life 147
Taking What Matters into My Own Hands 149
Primarily Sacrifice and Courage 151
Let's Talk about Sex 153
Which Is a Bigger Deal? 157
The Exchanged Life 161
The First Evidence of Change 164
If It's Worth Doing It's Worth Doing Badly 166
The Number One Indicator of Success in Life 168
Jesus Loved Judas 170
Take What You've Been Given and Pass It On 172
Pick Up Your Cross Daily and Follow Me 174
Stick It Out! 176
The Christian-Marriage Martyr 178
It's Not Good for Guys to Be Alone 181

TABLE OF CONTENTS

Maybe She's God's Tool? 183
Annoyances Are My Problem Not Hers 185
She's the Biggest Mistake of My Life 189

Conclusion 199
Bibliography 201

Foreword

I have known Don Fast for thirty years. I first met Don when we were both in youth ministry. Back then kids loved to listen to Don. He pulled no punches when he spoke. Those kids craved the God-given words that smacked them between the eyes and yet didn't leave them in despair whether they were the rebels or the rule followers (because he had been both). He is still doing that with adult "kids" who are married and need hope.

Again, Don pulls no punches. But his assessment is not bleak or hopeless. He knows divorce is not the solution. Nor does Don offer a weak Christianized answer that leads to frustration and failure.

Don gives hope, real hope. From a man who has made horrible choices, hurt others, and made life tough, then tried to tough it out and failed.

But God . . . (two of my favorite words in the Bible; see Eph 2:4–5). No matter the problem, I say, "But God . . ." God put Don where he can hear clearly, at the bottom. God changed Don's view of his "bad" wife. God asked him to die for his wife. Not by stepping in front of a bullet and going out heroically looking godly! But a slow death of giving up his unrealistic expectations of Laurie needing to meet his needs and his dreams for ministry and marriage. Yet, he is not bitter. How you ask? God worked in Don for him to know Christ as his source of fulfillment and has allowed God to change him. Don can speak to the unmet expectations that lead to disillusionment, despair, hopelessness, and divorce. Don can now speak to rising from that disillusionment to hope, purpose, restoration, fulfillment, and love.

No matter what your "bad" wife is like, God can give you the eyes to see her as he does: pure, holy, and lovely.

Read on and see if you have a "bad wife," as well. Then read some more to see if you are willing to get a new wife by having God transform . . . you.

G. Michael Wortham
Church elder and longtime friend

Preface

CHRIST IS THE CHRISTIAN life. There is no Christian life without Christ. He is the core; the center; the hub; the apex. Everything in the Christian life revolves around Him. The problems for many of us guys start after we finally meet her, "the love of our life," and our world begins to revolve around her instead of Him.

Second Corinthians 11:3 says, "But I am afraid that, as the serpent deceived Eve by his trickery, your minds will be led astray from sincere and pure devotion to Christ" (NASB). We are too easily distracted. Too easily "led astray" from our number one passion our number one love. My heart is an idol assembly line. It's unbelievably easy to turn a good thing into a bad idol. Our wives and marriages are really good things that too easily turn into idols.

Our idolatries are not our wife's fault. We have to be man enough to take responsibility for our choices and our chosen passions. That's what this little book is about: choices and chosen passions that have "led us astray from *our* sincere and pure devotion to Christ."

Psalms 16 says, "In Your presence is fullness of joy and at Your right hand are pleasures forever." Is there a possibility that your marital problems started when you chose to make being in her "presence" and at her "right hand" a higher priority than being in and at *His*?

The story is told of an old farmer and his longtime wife who were driving in his old bench-seated pickup. His wife made the comment, "I remember when we used to sit shoulder to shoulder

PREFACE

whenever we drove to town." The old farmer thought for a bit and then said, "I'm not the one who moved."

Jesus didn't move. You and I did. The goal of this little book is to get us to slide back over and return to that intimate love affair we used to have with our number one love and our truest passion, Jesus. As He gets Himself back into His rightful, soulmate spot, hopefully she will slide back to her "helpmate" spot.

I have a "bad" marriage.

Exodus 20:2

I don't need _____ in my "bad" marriage. I need *You*.

Isaiah 43:4

Why Write This?

The reason I'm writing this little book is because I believe God wants me to. Next, I have a "bad" marriage. My "bad" marriage is due to my being such an "idol factory" that I placed my wife, my plans, my marital fantasies ahead of Him. My goal is to take what I believe God has given me, what He has been putting me through in my "bad" marriage and, in His power, pass it on to you.

The problems, sufferings, disappointments, and challenges that are a common part of being married and the supernatural insights from the Bible are God's most powerful tools to make me more like Him and rid me of my long-held relational idols.

Proverbs 31:10; Psalm 119:9, 11

To Whom?

I believe the concepts in this book will work for women, but, because I'm a guy, I'm writing this to guys. My wife told me I should have written it to women instead of men, because I think more like a woman. Hmm? Anyway, I think the concepts will work for women, but I'm writing this for guys.

I am absolutely loved and a complete success.

John 17:23; Matthew 3:17

You Won't Be Able to Do This

You can't do marriage. You and I can't do anything that God designed and gave directions on how to do without Him doing it. That's the Christian life. That's the *exchanged life*. It's the Galatians 2:20 life: "My old self has been crucified with Christ. It is no longer I who live, but Christ lives in me. So I live in this earthly body by trusting in the Son of God, who loved me and gave himself for me."[1]

As you are reading this little book, please remember this, at the times you think you are doing marriage well, you may become either arrogant or self-righteous, thinking you can do it without God. When you're struggling in your marriage and see frequent and repeated failures, there's every likelihood you'll begin to blame, get angry, frustrated, and tired, and think of giving up or finding ways to cheat (there are lots of ways to cheat other than various types of affairs). This is not a self-help, task-oriented, DIY book. This is an *I can't on my own, but "I can" through Him, "do all things," including just loving my "bad" wife,* book (Phil 4:13).

---

1. All scripture quotations are from the New Living Translation unless otherwise noted.

"I can't. You never said I could. You can!
You always said You would."

Major W. Ian Thomas;[2] *Galatians 2:20*

---

2. From a lecture by Thomas on his book *Saving Grace* (Grace College of the Bible, 1979).

Motivational Verses

For over twenty years, I have seen God use a number of ideas I believe He's given me to share with the people I counsel in individual and group sessions. For a while now, new ideas on marriage started popping into my head. It seemed like quite a few of these new thoughts were far more intelligent and insightful than something I could come up with on my own. With that belief in mind, it seemed like I needed to take a chance and see if I could get some of these ideas out in book form to see if God would use them to help guys who are struggling in their marriages.

He has used a number of verses that have helped motivate and encourage me to get and keep going with this little writing project. A few of the verses are:

John 6:20: "Don't be afraid! It's okay! I'm here"! (This is now my favorite verse in the Bible)!

2 Thessalonians 1:11-12: "Pray that our God will make you fit for what He's called you to be, pray that He'll fill your good ideas and acts of faith with His own energy so that it all amounts to something. If your life honors the name of Jesus, He will honor you. Grace is behind and through all of this, our God giving Himself freely, the Master, Jesus Christ, giving Himself freely." The Message Translation

Acts 20:24: "My life is worth nothing to me unless I use it for finishing the work assigned me by the Lord Jesus-the work of telling others the good news about the wonderful grace of God."

Matthew 11:28-30: "Come to me, all of You who are weary and carry heavy burdens and I will give you rest. Take My yoke upon you. Let Me teach you, because I am humble and gentle, and you will find rest for your souls. For My yoke fits perfectly, and the burden I give you is light."

John 10:10: "I came that you might have life and have it to the full."

Jeremiah 1:4-10: "The Lord gave me this message: 'I knew you before I formed you in your mother's womb. Before you were born I set you apart and appointed you as my prophet to the nations.' 'O Sovereign Lord,' I said, 'I can't speak for you! I'm too young!' The Lord replied, 'Don't say, "I'm too young," for you must go wherever I send you and say whatever I tell you. And don't be afraid of the people, for I will be with you and will protect you. I, the Lord, have spoken!' Then the Lord reached out and touched my mouth and said, 'Look, I have put my words in your mouth! Today I appoint you to stand up against nations and kingdoms. Some you must uproot and tear down, destroy and overthrow. Others you must build up and plant.'"

Isaiah 43:1-5a: "But now, O Jacob, listen to the Lord who created you. O Israel, the one who formed you says, 'Do not be afraid, for I have ransomed you. I have called you by name; you are mine. When you go through deep waters, I will be with you. When you go through rivers of difficulty, you will not drown. When you walk through the fire of oppression, you will not be burned up; the flames will not consume you. For I am the Lord, your God, the Holy One of Israel, your Savior. I gave Egypt as a ransom for your freedom; I gave Ethiopia and Seba in your place. Others were given in exchange for you. I traded their lives for yours because you are precious to me. You are honored, and I love you. Do not be afraid, for I am with you.'"

Lamentations 3:21:, ". . . Dare to hope!"

Zechariah 8:9: ". . . Finish the task."

"If it weren't for the people I've met (Jesus) and the books I've read (the Bible), I'd be unchanged during my lifetime."

—*Me*

Helpful Books to Consider Reading

1. From the Bible: Psalms, Proverbs, Hosea, Habakkuk, John, Romans (3–5), 2 Corinthians, Galatians, Ephesians, Philippians, and Colossians
2. *The Indwelling Life of Christ*, by Maj. Ian Thomas
3. *Trusting God*, by Jerry Bridges
4. *Because He Loves Me*, by Elyse Fitzpatrick
5. *Foxe's Book of Martyrs*, by John Foxe
6. *Triumphing over Sinful Fear*, by Johns Flavel
7. *Hinds' Feet on High Places*, by Hannah Hurnard
8. *Counterfeit Gods*, by Tim Keller
9. *The Meaning of Marriage*, by Tim Keller and Kathy Keller

I surrender. I want what *You* want.

Jeremiah 39:17–20

A Little Background

I am sixty-three years old. Jesus began living inside me back in 1977 when I realized I was a sinner and that He died on the cross, rose from the dead, and did this all for me because I was helpless, hopeless, and spiritually dead.

I came from a massively messed up, spiritually abusive family that had lots of rules, very little love, and even less forgiveness (my family is made up of professional resentment-keepers, including me). Two years after becoming a Christian, I went to Bible college, eventually graduated, and afterward stayed on staff with the college for a couple years. I then spent the next decade or so doing full-time youth pastor–like work with several churches and Christian ministries. I then got married to my gracious wife, Laurie, (more on that later), went back to school to get some counseling/discipleship skills, and after graduation served as a head pastor for about a year.

The year prior to serving as pastor, our son Sammy, who is now twenty-three, was born three-and-a-half months premature. He was diagnosed with chronic lung disease and significant cerebral palsy. Sammy's challenges at birth and pressures from being a newlywed and new pastor exposed what a self-centered, immature, and controlling person I was and still am.

Due to all the additional stress, my lack of character, maturity, and not knowing how to hand stuff off to Jesus, my wife very healthfully divorced me. Seven years later we were remarried, by God's amazing grace, and have been working through our second attempt at "whom God has put together" for almost fifteen years now.

I wanted you to know what my background is. I have found that many of the "professionals" have lots of good and biblical things to say but get pretty fussy when it comes to sharing their struggles, timelines, and failures. The cool thing I see from scripture is that God has a tendency to use the failed, the flawed, and the fallen, because that's all there are (Rom 3:23; 1 Cor 1:26; 1 Tim 1:12–17). I wonder if the best helpers are wounded recoverers? Those who have been through it and supernaturally got through it (2 Cor 1:1–6; Heb 4:14–16).

Thank you for taking the time and spending the money to check out what God has shown this "worst of sinners," me.

I live for *You*, not her.

Luke 14:26

This Is Not One of Those Books

I hear pastors, speakers, "experts" present all their by-the-book, how-it's-supposed-to-be, Bible-based guidelines of the dos and don'ts of Christian marriage. I don't disagree with what they are saying. The question I have is, "What if I'm not there?" What if I am not who I'm supposed to be, where I'm supposed to be, or how I'm supposed to be as an Ephesians 5 Christian husband? What do I do in the middle of the not-there-yets? Do I keep beating that marital "dead horse"? Do I keep marinating in the pain, suffering, dissatisfaction, unbiblicalness, and imperfections of my "bad" marriage? What's a messed-up boy supposed to do?

I have dozens of how-to, relational, marriage, dating, and love-language books that I've been reading since 1987. They promote that men and women are from different planets, and that one prefers respect and the other needs love, etc., etc. But the bottom line is, I can't live out what all the "experts" are pushing. And I could be wrong, and I could be jaded, and could be a "glass-half-empty" kinda guy, but I wonder how many of them are putting into practice what they are all preaching?

That's the reason for this book. I want to promote the possibility that our "bad" marriages will never look completely like God said marriage was supposed to look like. And I wonder if biblical grace says that's okay? I want to push the fact that God arranges and blesses imperfect marriages. Why? Because that's all there are. No matter what the experts are saying, no matter how many Bible verses they give to support what they just wrote, there ain't no such thing as a perfect marriage or perfect couple. Anybody can look good standing in front of an audience, or behind a closed door, but what's going on behind the scenes when nobody else is looking?

Every single marriage needs grace. A grace that says, "I love you just the way you are, not the way you (two) or anyone else says you should be."

That doesn't mean there can't be growth and change. But I wonder if there's something more important than growth or change? What about love and acceptance in the middle of the imperfection? What about "I know who you are and what you did, and I still love you." And "even if you never change, because I'm a complete screwup and Jesus continues to love me in the middle of all my screwed-up-ness, with Him living in and through me, I'm gonna pass that same love and acceptance on to you, my 'bad' wife."

One of the major problems with real change is, if it's going to happen, God's going to be the one who does it. If it happens at all, it takes a really long time and has to have a very special environment in order to take place. That environment is forgiveness, love, and acceptance. Change occurs best in an atmosphere of God's love and acceptance.

Bottom line, there will always be struggles and biblical deformities in our marriages. So, what do you do in the middle of the "badness," brokenness, imperfections, and unbiblical-nesses of your marriage? Grace! Paraphrasing Paul's words from Romans 7:24–25, "Oh, what a miserable *husband* I am! Who will free me from my *husbanding* that is dominated by sin and death? Thank God! The answer for my 'bad' marriage is in Jesus Christ our Lord."

All that to say, this book is not one of those books. This book is primarily about improving your relationship with Jesus. Through God's power making Him your number one passion, not her. With the happy potential by-product of improving your relationship with your "bad" wife.

I can't believe You know every little detail about me and yet still unconditionally love me. Oh Jesus, please pass this same love from You to me, onto my "bad" wife through me.

1 John 4:7-11

The Relational Iceberg

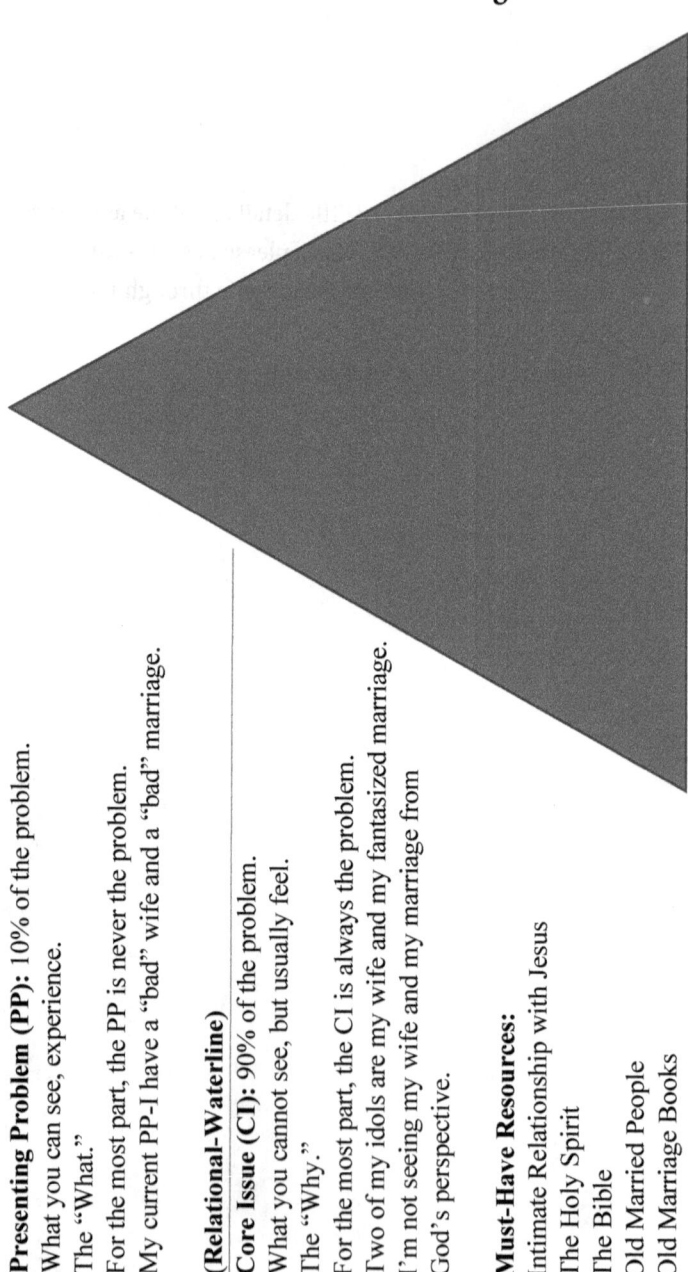

Presenting Problem (PP): 10% of the problem.
What you can see, experience.
The "What."
For the most part, the PP is never the problem.
My current PP-I have a "bad" wife and a "bad" marriage.

(Relational-Waterline)

Core Issue (CI): 90% of the problem.
What you cannot see, but usually feel.
The "Why."
For the most part, the CI is always the problem.
Two of my idols are my wife and my fantasized marriage.
I'm not seeing my wife and my marriage from God's perspective.

Must-Have Resources:
Intimate Relationship with Jesus
The Holy Spirit
The Bible
Old Married People
Old Marriage Books

Idolatry isn't just being disloyal to God, it's jumping in "bed" with something or someone other than God.

Hosea 1:2

"Bad" Marriages

So, what's a "bad" marriage? For most of us guys, the above-the-relational-waterline view is gonna look something like constant arguing, having "nothing in common," little or no sex, little or no communication, "you've lost that lovin' feelin'," "irreconcilable differences," "you spend too much," "you make too high a priority of your family," nitpicking—the "what have you done for me lately," "50/50" relationship stuff, or the ever-popular "I love you, I'm just not in love with you" junk.

These thoughts/beliefs are the *whats* of relational discord, not the *whys*. All the "bad" stuff I just suggested, in one form or another, can be identified in a "bad" marriage. The problem is that none of these thoughts/beliefs are the problem. These thoughts/beliefs are the low-hanging, relationally dysfunctional fruit that's easy to "see," but are just symptoms of the relational problem, not the problem. These PPs (presenting problems) keep us busy, and most likely frustrated and tired, but in the end, PPs don't make a dent in where we need to get in our "bad" marriages.

The *whats* in this illustration might be ten percent (at best) of the real problem. An example of a ten percent PP is anger. Anger is extremely easy to see, feel, and express, but not the real problem or CI (core issue). The *why* or underlying cause (CI) of anger could be an unhealthy need for control due to shame, confusion, and/or fear. If you choose to focus on the *what* of anger, you'll spend a lot of time and energy on the symptom of the real issue, but most likely you won't get anywhere.

Whys on the other hand in this illustration are the big deal. They're where you want to go when identifying what to sacrifice on God's altar (more on that later). The real relational stuff that needs

JUST LOVE HER

to be worked on is below the relational waterline. This is where the CI(s) and ninety percent or more of the real sin resides. CIs are many times felt, but most of the time superficially diagnosed from a *what* rather than a God-identified *why* perspective. *Whys* are the root, *whats* are the fruit. *Whys* are the fire. *Whats* are the smoke. *Whys* whisper. *Whats* scream. The "screaming" and in-your-face observing of *whats* make it easy to get distracted and stay above the relational waterline rather than diving beneath the "surface" in order to get to the real CI, or *why*, of the relational problem(s).

Many guys don't want to dive below the relational waterline. It's almost as if, if they were to go there, they'd be admitting there are serious problems in their marriage, and they don't want to make that admission. It's almost as if they're saying, "Relational ignorance is bliss." No. Relational ignorance/avoidance is an affair or a divorce waiting to happen, not bliss.

To get to a place where we get the big boys of change involved, those boys being God, Jesus, the Holy Spirit, and the Bible, we're going to want to put our "bad" marriage off to the side and literally on a daily basis say, "Jesus please be my number one passion and love. Please take away any and all idols that I have placed in front of You, even if it is my 'bad' wife and my 'bad' marriage. I want You more than anything else." God will answer this prayer. This will not be easy, and this prayer, when answered, is full of pain. The sad part is, most of us guys run from God-crafted pain, rather than thanking Him for it and what it's doing for me and my "bad" marriage.

To get the right work done down there (below the relational waterline), we'll have to shift focus. Our "bad" wives and our "bad" marriages will have to take a relational back seat. The main priority below the relational waterline will be to make a priority of our primary love relationship, Jesus. As we're focusing on Him, our number one priority will be to experience His love, grace, acceptance, and forgiveness. Full stop. "Do not pass Go. Do not collect your relational $200." The goal is to stop, marinate in His love, grace, acceptance, and forgiveness while sitting at Jesus' feet, and make it my number one priority to know Him, be loved by Him, and have

Him be my/your number one passion not her (Luke 10:38–42). When this begins to happen, she will no longer be your number one PP and you'll now have the love you're experiencing from Him to pass on to her.

So why all the hubbub about *whats* and *whys*? Because the goal of this entire chapter is to get us to think below the relational waterline. To not get tricked by what we see, feel, or experience, or by the Christian self-help tricks and techniques many of the "professionals" have been pushing for decades. The goal here is to keep our eyes on Jesus. We all, me included, are so easily distracted from our true number one passion, our true number one love, Jesus. Second Corinthians 11:3 says, "But I fear that somehow your pure and undivided devotion to Christ will be corrupted, just as Eve was deceived by the cunning ways of the serpent" (NASB).

I'm going to ask you to keep this relational iceberg illustration in mind as you read this book. Every time you see "bad" wife and "bad" marriage throughout this presentation, I'm not saying that they and it are literally bad. What I'm hoping you'll do, every time you see "bad" attached to wife and marriage, is to stop thinking what you're currently thinking. Your "bad" wife and your "bad" marriage are not bad from a biblical perspective—or from God's perspective. Our wives are what you and I need. They are our perfect gifts from Jesus. They are not the problem. They are our "dearest treasure" (Jer 16:5)—the God-given "wife of your youth" (Prov 16:5). The goal is to get us to start seeing our "bad" wives as God-ordained instruments to get rid of our relational idols and be more in love with Him—and eventually our wives.

"How much better is marital wisdom than gold, and relational understanding than silver!"

Paraphrase of Proverbs 16:16

The *Whys* of My "Bad" Marriage

1. Jesus doesn't live inside of you (Rom 8:9).

2. If He does live inside of you, you have a superficial, performance-oriented, do-more, try-harder, pious self-denial relationship with Jesus. A relationship where you're trusting more in what you do for Him instead of resting in what He has already done for you.

3. Jesus is not your number one passion (2 Cor 11:3; Phil 3:8).

4. Due to your superficial or nonexistent relationship with Jesus, you have a "God-shaped vacuum" (Pascal).

5. This God-shaped vacuum hurts (spiritual loneliness is painful).

6. Due to the chronic and/or acute pain you're currently experiencing due to your nonexistent, plastic/placebo, performance-oriented, superficial relationship with Jesus, you run after "little-*g*" gods or smaller-than-God-replacements in order to stop the God-shaped vacuum pain.

7. These smaller-than-God things are called idols. Idols work until they don't (eventually, they always don't). When you run after them instead of Him, it's called idolatry.

8. As a man, your primary idols will usually be your work or your wife (we're going to focus on the second in this little book).

9. Your relational idolatry takes place when you run to your wife to get your primary needs met instead of to Jesus.

10. Much of the stuff that's called love is actually idolatry (sinful taking, rather than giving).

11. Most of the problems in your "bad" marriage are initially due to selfishnesses stemming from relational, unrealistic expectations and fantasies. Your hope (demand) is that she will give you what you never got but always wanted. In your mind, she is your relational ticket to bypass God, because He's not making you feel the way you want to feel, when you want to feel it. This eventually expresses itself in your relational idolatries. Thus, the need for this book.

She is my help mate. *He* is my soulmate

Genesis 2:18; Psalm 42:2

"Bad" Wife Identifiers

1. A "bad" wife is that person I said "I do" to, with the goal of getting from her what only God can give. But because she's not God and can't give it, she is a "bad" wife.
2. A "bad" wife is a "bad" wife because I had expectations of her that she would supply for me those things that either God wouldn't give me or has been in the process of taking from me due to their sinful or idolatrous nature. Since she's not meeting my unrealistic demands in this area, she is a "bad" wife.
3. A "bad" wife is a "bad" wife because after all my years of failed attempts at running after my smaller-than-God things to fill my "God-shaped vacuum," she is my next attempt, but since she's not able to fill my God-shaped vacuum either, she's a "bad" wife.
4. A "bad" wife is a "bad" wife because she did not meet my unrealistic expectations of making me feel less lonely and less incomplete (the silly, but much-loved phrase from Jerry McGuire, "You complete me"); she, therefore, is a "bad" wife.
5. A "bad" wife is a "bad" wife because due to the chronic pain of my "God-shaped vacuum," I pieced together a fantasized female that I would marry, from the movies, songs, books, relational experiences, and mommy issues I have. This patched-together fantasy female is so fantastic, so unrealistic, so unachievable that even if God had a wife (which He obviously doesn't), she wouldn't be able to meet my unrealistic relational expectations. She, therefore, is a "bad" wife.

6. A "bad" wife is a "bad" wife because she is unable to meet my many times unspoken and unknown (by me) demands to fill my God-shaped vacuum. She, therefore, is a "bad" wife.

7. A "bad" wife is a "bad" wife because she is an unrecognized (on my part), God-tool, that God has been using in my life to take away my idols and make me more like Him. The problem is that this God-process hurts, and instead of loving, accepting, and being grateful for her and her part in His God-crafted plan, she is a "bad" wife.

8. Is there a possibility that she is a "bad" wife because I'm expecting her to do for me what I stopped believing God would or could? God didn't do it on my timetable, so now it's her turn. It's now obvious that she can't meet those same sinful demands. She, therefore, is a "bad" wife.

9. Is there a possibility that she's a "bad" wife because my control-freak-ness wants to feel the way I want to feel, when I want to feel it, but since God hasn't met my demands in this area, on my timetable, she now has to, but is unable to, because God never designed her to? Therefore, she's a "bad" wife.

Jesus and God were glorified when Jesus followed through on the plan to *just love us*. God will be glorified through us, as we, in His power, follow through on His plan to *just love her*.

John 3:16; 12:27–32; 13:31–32; 16:33;
Revelation 3:21

Grace?

In order to make any of the stuff I'm promoting in this book work, you're going to need to come to the realization that all of it is completely impossible without God's grace. The problem is, and this is massively embarrassing, I don't know what to say about grace. I have studied it, I have listened to sermons about it, I would say that I am absolutely dependent on and ridiculously infatuated, in love with it, but without copying and plagiarizing others, I don't know what to say about grace.

What I can say is, without grace I'd be in hell. Without grace, my wife wouldn't have married and remarried me. Without grace, I can't get out of bed. Without grace, I can't floss my teeth. Without grace, I can't think straight. Without grace, I can't stand people. Without grace, I can't return love to Jesus. Without grace, I couldn't write this little book. Without grace, God couldn't look at me and Jesus couldn't love me. Without grace, I'm hopeless and helpless. Grace is amazing!

With grace, there's hope. With grace, God forgave me. With grace, my wife loves and accepts me. With grace, my son is still alive. With grace, I didn't kill myself. With grace, God has loved and used me. With grace, I'm not stuck in my past. With grace, when I'm weak, He's strong. With grace, stuff that's impossible is possible. With grace, I can be authentically grateful for and in love with my "bad" wife in our "bad" marriage. Oh Jesus, thank You for Your grace!

Biblically speaking, where in the Bible does it say that marriage's primary priority is my satisfaction and fulfillment *(the chief end of man . . . Westminster Shorter Catechism)*?

Accepting the "Bad" with the Good

This ain't heaven. It's not utopia. It's not even Disney World! We live on Planet Death. At best, we are two broken people, working through our brokenness, in broken ways, on a broken planet. While living on our broken planet, working through our broken relationship, in broken ways, most of us are lucky we haven't gotten strangled yet. If you're like me, in light of all the dumb stuff I've said and done over the past multiple years, we're pretty fortunate to not be missing various body parts. Long story made short, nothing is perfect on Planet Death. That's why perfectionism, the inability to accept the bad with the good, is so devastating to our "bad" marriages.

Perfectionism flows from the perfectionist. Perfectionism crushes and sucks the life out of anyone who comes in contact with or is in relationship with the perfectionist. Perfectionism demands that the relational peas can't touch the relational potatoes. If they do, the entire relational plate has to be thrown out. Even though there's perfectly good pork chops, gravy, and biscuits on the relational plate along with the perfectly good peas and potatoes; because the two touched, the "bad" has tarnished the good and now everything is "bad." That's perfectionism.

The perfectionist feels perfectly good when they're doing good, and perfectly bad when they're doing bad. There is very little, if any middle ground. The perfectionist has a tendency to blame and condemn the initially perfect other (they looked perfect before the perfectionist actually got to know them), but now having gotten to know them (the now less-than-perfect other), has touched the relational peas one too many times and now has to either be "fixed" or "thrown away." Most of the time "fixing" comes in the form of holding resentments and reminding the less-than-perfect other of their many perceived (perfectionist's perception), failings from last week, last month, last year, or thirty years ago. The throwing away comes in the form of divorce, affairs, comparisons with past previously perfect others, substance use, pornography, silent treatments, workaholism, excessive hobbies, etc.

When someone has the sin of perfectionism, they demand perfection, first of all from themselves, eventually from everything and everybody, including, obviously their "bad" wife. The problem with perfectionism/perfection, it's impossible to attain. Perfection many times ends up being an attempt to make up for a sin, fault, or weakness in some area of the perfectionist's life. They see that they're broken and imperfect and have experienced some form of pain due to their imperfections and in attempt to make up for those imperfections and escape future pain, they knowingly or unknowingly strive for perfection in order to either cover-up or compensate for their persistent imperfections.

Perfectionism is a painful, overextended, mental/emotional pendulum swing that goes far beyond trying to do your best, to having to be the best. Doing your best isn't good enough for the perfectionist. One perfectionistic phrase promoted by Dale Earnhardt was "second place is the first loser." Everybody loved Dale Earnhardt, and initially this phrase sounded kinda cool. But in reality second place is just second place. The drive to always be first and never second is impossible to attain and eventually just makes you tired and worse.

Most professionals would probably blame this problem on parenting. I'm not so sure. It seems like nowadays, if anything's wrong with anybody, it's the parents' fault. If you're reading this book, you're probably at the age where it's more reasonable for you to be responsible for your own sins and character flaws, not mom and dad. I'm not exactly sure where this problem came from, but I wonder if it might have something to do with the fall?

Back in the day when Adam and Eve were walking around Eden, I seriously doubt before Adam bit the fruit that perfectionism was even a thing. Perfection yes. Perfectionism no. It's kind of

Just Love Her

like a fish thinking about water. When the little guy is swimming around in it, most likely he takes it for granted. When, for whatever reason he's out of it, Mr. Fishy's definitely going to be thinking a lot about it. I wonder if that's what happened to us. Romans 5:12–19, specifically v. 12, says that when Adam sinned, we all sinned. Maybe because of Adam's screwup, and by spiritual extension, we all screwed up, i.e., sinned with him, we've been looking for our lost perfection just like Mr. Fishy's lost water?

This is where grace comes in. For the most part, every one of us knows how we're supposed to be. The problem is none of us is who we're "supposed" to be. Everyone, from our parents, teachers, Sunday school teachers, preachers, police officers, even commercials, have told us how we're supposed to be, but we're just not. When we're able to be honest, we see ourselves as miserable persons, obviously less than perfect, trying to act as if we're perfect in front of other less than perfect persons who are faking it just like us.

Who can save us from this life of imperfection? Paraphrasing Paul in Romans 7:24, "Oh, what a miserable husband I am! Who will free me from this life permeated with marital imperfections?"

We have at least two choices when it comes to addressing our imperfections. We can attempt the hopeless task of creating our own perfection through our own performance (Rom 3:23; Gal 3), or we can rest in and rely on Jesus' imputed (spiritual deposit in our spiritual "bank account") perfection for us (Rom 5:1).

So, then, what's the fix for perfectionism? Its only cure is grace. Grace in this case is a no-strings-attached, free gift from God that says, "I love you just the way you are, not the way you or anyone else says you should be. You are perfect! Right now." Romans 5:1–2 says, "Therefore, since we have been justified [that is, acquitted of sin, declared blameless before God] by faith, [let us grasp the fact that] we have peace with God [and the joy of reconciliation with Him] through our Lord Jesus Christ (the Messiah, the Anointed). Through Him we also have access by faith into this [remarkable state of] grace in which we [firmly and safely and securely] stand. Let us rejoice in our hope and the confident

Just Love Her

assurance of [experiencing and enjoying] the glory of [our great] God [the manifestation of His excellence and power]" (Amplified Bible).

So, the primary way of undoing perfectionism is to take a passages like Romans 5; Ephesians 1; Ephesians 3:14–21; Hebrews 10, and countless others, and acknowledge that these verses are the spiritual "lenses" that God "looks" through to evaluate us. When God looks at us, He doesn't evaluate us based on our sinful, imperfections, but rather Jesus' "it is finished," perfect work on the cross for us (John 17:23; Eph 1:22).

Most people when they finally recognize their imperfections, and are able to authentically admit they have this perfectionism thing, just try harder. I call this the Do-More-Try-Harder Syndrome or the Pious-Self-Denial Syndrome. The problem with these two extremes is like Paul in Romans 7, the problem gets worse and they get a lot more tired, but no more perfect (Col 2:21–23).

Grace on the other hand says, "I can't. You never said I could. You can. You always said you would."[3] The only way to get rid of perfectionism is to get out of the way, stop trying, and start resting (Isa 30:15). Resting in what God has already done for us on the cross. It's called grace.

So, wrapping this section up; how can we get rid of our perfectionism and our struggles with accepting the "bad" in our "bad" wives, and our "bad" marriages? The answer: rest in and rely on what God has already done for us and them in making us "pure and holy and without fault" (Col 1:22). Then rest in the fact that Jesus said that God loves us as much as God loves Him (John 17:23). Now take the reality that God's love has made you perfect in His eyes, and with that reality get off the perfectionistic treadmill and leave yourself and your "bad" wife alone. Marinate in Isaiah 30:15, which reads, "Only in returning to Me and resting in Me will you be saved." There you have it. That's how you accept the "bad" with the good.

---

3. Thomas, *Saving Life*, class notes.

The second I experience excruciating pain from my sin-filled thoughts of my "bad" wife and my "bad" marriage, it's time to worship! (If need be, write down ten passion-filled characteristics of God that you are passionately overwhelmed with on a 3 x 5 card, break it out, and worship Him.)
Take your eyes off her and worship Him.

Psalm 95:6–7

"You make plans that are contrary to Mine."

Isaiah 30:1; Mark 10:8–9; Luke 7:23

"The Lord will work out His plans for my life."
Which is much better than the plans I had for my "bad" marriage.

Psalm 138:7a; Luke 7:23

Offended by My "Bad" Marriage?

He was given God's plan for his life before he was ever born. He only had one job description for his life. He held that same position his entire life. He had confirmation of his profession before he was even born. He was given supernatural affirmation of his predetermined career path while practicing it from the power player of all time, identify him as, "the greatest man that ever lived." John the Baptist had a pretty cool resume! And then Luke 7 happened?

John was doing what he was supposed to do. He was practicing his predetermined profession of announcing the coming of the Messiah. And then we find out from Matthew 14 that John got slammed in jail for confronting a local, high-ranking political leader of the immoral relationship he was having with his brother's wife. Something about John's being placed behind bars "offended" him. We know this because in the Luke 7 passage, Jesus, while talking about John, said, "Blessed is anyone who does not take offense at Me." What does that mean? How does the guy, who Jesus said was the greatest guy who ever lived, get offended by the Guy who gave him that title? Let's check it out.

Looking back to Luke 1, when the unborn Jesus and his mom, Mary, visit Mary's aunt Elizabeth, John, who is also unborn at this time, jumped while still in his mom's womb. It seems like John was somehow supernaturally notified of, and as a result, got excited about, his cousin Jesus' visit. Elizabeth was also apparently excited and was prompted by the Holy Spirit to sing a song expressing how blessed Mary was to be the mother of the Messiah (Luke 1:39–45).

From before his birth, John had confirmation that God's plan for his life was for him to announce his cousin Jesus as the long-awaited Messiah. It wouldn't be hard to imagine that while John was growing up, both of his parents would've reminded him of not only the angel Gabriel's announcement of his mother's supernatural, old-age pregnancy, but also of Isaiah 40 (they didn't have chapters and verses back then, but you get where I'm going here), prophesying God's plan for John's life. Every time John heard his name, he would have been reminded of God's plan for his life; knowing that God through that angel gave him his name, which was outside of his ancestral bloodline. His parents would've reminded him that he was filled with the Holy Spirit before he was born; that he couldn't drink alcohol and would have the "spirit of Elijah" to help him with the predetermined plan God had for his life. His entire life was lived with one purpose and one purpose only, to fulfill God's plan of announcing the coming Messiah.

Further confirmation that John was accomplishing the God-directed plan for his life was in Matthew 3, where the passage says, "'The heavens were opened, and he [John] saw the Spirit of God descending like a dove and settling on Him [Jesus]. And a voice from heaven that said, 'This is my dearly loved Son, who brings Me great joy'" (v. 17). Seriously! Would anyone need any further confirmation identifying the reality that you were following God's plan for your life?

John was absolutely convinced, while receiving frequent, supernatural confirmations, that what he was doing was God's plan for his life. While John was riding the wave of success, crowds attending his crusades, and having God, Jesus, and the Holy Spirit in attendance, he was convinced that he was doing God's will and this was God's plan for his life. The "offending" came when the success and confirmations stopped, and the incarcerations started.

I wonder if John's "offense" came when God's plan for John's life stopped looking like John's plan for John's life?

I wonder if John's confusing "offendedness" toward Jesus can be traced back to two of John's statements when he said, "You are the One" (Matt 3:14), and later "Are you the One?" (Luke 7:19). Is there a possibility that John's "offense" toward Jesus was a byproduct of John making a priority of John's plans for John's life over Jesus' plans for John's life?

I wonder if the "offending" was due to the possibility that John hadn't factored into his plan for his life the pain and suffering that God had planned for John's life? Trying to keep it even more simple, is there a possibility that John got confused and "offended" when John's life got hard?

I wonder if John's confusion began to appear when it seemed like God stopped blessing John's plan for John's life? The hard part came when what John thought was God's plan for his life stopped looking like what John had planned for John's life. John may have planned on being in power with Jesus when He overthrew the invading Roman government. I don't know. Whatever John's plan for his life was, it apparently did not include being jailed and/or beheaded. And since God's plan wasn't matching up with John's plan, John got "offended."

The *Theological Dictionary of the New Testament* suggests the word *offended* here in the original means to "lose confidence in."[4] I wonder if what Jesus is saying here is, "Blessed, or happy or fortunate, are those who, when life gets hard, gets scary and confusing and stops looking like what you thought it was supposed to look like, don't lose confidence in Me and My plan for your life. Don't get upset or annoyed or pick up an offense toward Me because My plan for your life stopped looking like your plan for your life."

So, what does John's confusion, offense, and lack of trust in Jesus' plan for his life have to do with my "bad" marriage? The correlation looks like this. When you first met her and everything was new, exciting, and going well, you were absolutely convinced that she was "the one" that would fulfill "God's" plan for your life. As long as she was fulfilling that plan you made for what marriage was supposed to look like, she was obviously the one that God planned for you to marry.

Now that marriage has gotten hard and she is no longer satisfying you and appears to be blowing up your plan for how your marriage was supposed to look, you're "offended." You've now moved from "You are the one" to "Are you the one?" Just like John. Like John, you lost confidence in God's plan for your marriage

---

4. Kittel, *Theological Dictionary*, 1039.

when it stopped being satisfying, easy, and fulfilling and no longer looked like the plan you had for your marriage.

So, here's the point. Just because marriage got hard doesn't change the fact that this is God's plan for your "bad" marriage. The offense comes when you make a higher priority of your plan for your marriage over God's plan for your marriage. Like John, if you're experiencing confusion, pain, loneliness, and a bunch of other junk that's blowing up your pre-fantasized plans of marriage, is there a possibility that all that confusion, pain, and loneliness was actually and always a part of God's plan for your marriage (Phil 1:29; 3:10b; John 9:1–3)?

We get ourselves in trouble when we start believing the pablum that love and marriage should be easy, fulfilling, second nature, something that "shouldn't be this hard." Here's a little secret: marriage is hard. Wouldn't it be reasonable to believe that the hardest thing in life (marriage) is going to be hard? We get offended when we think it should be easy, natural, and something other than what it is right now, hard. Is there a possibility that, like John, hard was a part of God's plan for your life and more specifically, your "bad" marriage?

Just for the fun of it, in contrast to John, Paul is an example of not getting "offended" by God's plan for his life. Like John, Paul was shown God's plan for his life in advance (Gal 1, 2; Acts 9). One difference might be that Paul knew ahead of time that it was going to be hard and would include suffering. One of the first things God said about Paul through Ananias is, "I will show him [Paul] how much he must suffer for My name" (Acts 9:16).

God's plan for Paul was full of hard. I mean all kinds of hard. He got beaten, shipwrecked, seriously cold, went without food, was beat up by both Gentiles and Jews, got stoned, and got placed in jail just like John. But here's the major difference, Paul was more committed to God's plan for Paul's life than Paul's plan for Paul's life. During Paul's incarceration, he wrote half the New Testament and shared the gospel with the guards who were guarding him (Phil 1:13). Paul didn't get offended. He, through God's power, just continued God's plan in the middle of the potentially "offending" circumstances.

Whose plan for your life and marriage are you more committed to, Gods or yours? If it's yours, you're going to get offended. You will become confused, you will lose confidence in, and hold resentments toward God and your "bad" wife. If you are offended at God and your "bad" marriage, it's because you're hanging onto your plan and being ticked at His.

Matthew 16:25 says, "If you try to hang on to your life, you will lose it. But if you give up your life for My sake, you will save it." I'd like to paraphrase it in the context of God's plan for your "bad" marriage. "If you try to hang on to your plan for your marriage, you will lose it. But if you give up your plan for your marriage for My sake, you will save it." Paul is an example of "giving up" his plan for his life for the sake of Jesus' plan for his life. You're going to want to do the same if you want to keep from getting offended by your "bad" marriage.

Thank You for loving me so much that You considered me worthy to receive this gift of suffering in my "bad" marriage.

Acts 5:41; Philippians 1:29; 3:10b; Hebrews 12:5–6

Did God Really Put Us Together?

In Mark 10:9, Jesus says, "Therefore what God has joined together, let no one separate." So, here's a simple question, did God really put you two together?

It was easy, in the early stages of the dating process. Twitterpation had set in, she was "perfect," the "total package," and you "worshiped the ground she walked on." Hassles were few; fun and excitements were many. Even if you thought you did, you didn't really know her.

So what? How could something that felt this good possibly be "bad?" She had to be "the one." All the relational stars had aligned, she was obviously God's choice for you.

Ah, but now there's now. The problem is, now there's problems. What used to be easy is now hard. Life and marriage now seem to be the opposite of when you were dating. Hassles are many; fun and excitements are few. Responsibilities. Responsibilities. Responsibilities. Everything was supposed to get better after you said, "I do." She was supposed to take away all your negative, empty, and unwanted feelings. The problem is, she didn't. Life seems to have gotten harder not easier after marriage.

You and I both know that Paul said it would be this way (1 Cor 7). But your twitterpation was obviously more authoritative than what God and Paul had to say. And now, after marriage, your hopes, expectations, and fantasies aren't panning out. You think, "It's gotta be her. I was doing fine before I met her. Did God really put us together?"

Question: Does God ever have a plan B? Has God, in His sovereignty, providence, and omnipotence, ever had one of His plans thwarted? The obvious answer is no.

Proverbs 16 has these wonderful "no-plan-B" verses (1, 3, 9, 33). Verse 9 says, "We can make our plans, but the Lord determines our steps." Obviously, we are the ones who said yes. We're the ones who said, "I do." But according to v. 9 and many others, God was the One determining our relational steps. He was the One determining the dating process. He was the One determining us asking the "big question." He was the One "determining," us walking down the aisle. He was the One "determining" us saying, "I do." He was the One who "determined" that we be the two whom He put together in marriage (Mark 10:9).

And if all these "determinings" are true, is there a possibility the hard times you're currently going through were also a part of His "determinings" in your "bad" marriage?

So, in the context of God's sovereignty, providence, and omnipotence, just because your marriage got hard doesn't mean God didn't "determine" it. Just because the twitterpation didn't last, doesn't mean God didn't "determine" it. Just because she hurt you, doesn't mean God didn't "determine" it. Just because _____ happened, doesn't mean God didn't "determine" it. Just because _____ didn't happen doesn't mean God didn't "determine" it. The presence of negatives or the absence of positives do not determine God's "determinings." We have to stop looking at our preconceived ideas of what our marital circumstances were supposed to look like, and surrender to the fact that He's in charge and, yes, *He did really put us together.*

Hebrews 12:2 says that "for the joy set before Him, He endured the cross." Why is it so easy for us to believe it was God's "determinings" for Jesus to go through hard times, but at the same time question if it's God's "determinings" when we go through them? We place far too much faith in our feelings. Just because something got hard doesn't mean it's not God's will, not part of His "determinings" (John 9:1–3). Just because my marriage is "bad," doesn't mean it isn't God's plan A. My positive emotions or lack of them do not determine God's "determinings" for me. Just because I don't feel the way I felt when we were dating doesn't mean God didn't determine this.

JUST LOVE HER

You may have heard the phrase "Don't change horses in the middle of the stream." Or "don't doubt in the dark what God showed you in the light." Just because relational difficulties have disturbed, derailed, or "offended" your pre-fantasized plan of what your marriage was supposed to look like doesn't mean God made a mistake. Is there a possibility that your pre-fantasized marital plan, was actually idolatrous? Whom God has put together, let no man, not even me or you, separate.

If I knew what You knew, I'd ask for what You put us through.
If I knew what You knew, I'd ask for what we're going through.
If I knew what You knew, I'd ask for what we will go through.

Jeremiah 29:11; Romans 8:28; Mark 10:9

Everybody Plays Broken

It was a while ago, so I'm not sure I'm getting all the specifics right. But I was watching one of the major sports reporting shows and one of the analysts was talking about how injuries affect every professional football player throughout the season. I don't remember anything else he said other than a quote he said his father passed on to him. It went something like, "Everybody plays broken."

I've rumbled that quote around in my head for years. And as I have, I believe the intent of his father's thought is true not only in professional football, but in life as well. In one way or another everybody plays broken.

One of the problems with most people, outside of the gridiron, is that much of the time throughout their lives, they don't recognize they're playing broken. Jesus in Mark 2:17 said, "Those who are healthy have no need of a physician, but [only] those who are sick; I did not come to call the righteous, but sinners [who recognize their sin and humbly seek forgiveness]."

The simple truth I want to get across in this section is that Jesus came for the broken. For years I've believed, based on this and other similar passages from the Bible, that there are two types of people, the sick and the healthy, the broken and unbroken. But that's not true. There's actually only one type of person. That one type is broken. All of us are sick and all of us are broken (Rom 3:10, 23). The problem comes when we don't "recognize" it.

There are at least three types of broken people. First, and the most difficult of the three, are those who are broken and sick but believe they're healthy. The sickest and most broken of this first category are those who are so sick and broken that they see you as broken, as the one with the problem, not themselves. If you were to attempt to point out their problem, they in their brokenness make you the problem. "I'm not broken. You are" (Matt 19:21–22; Luke 7:36–49).

Second are those who are broken and won't admit it. An example of this would be the older brother in the parable of the "prodigal son" in Luke 15. And finally, there are those who are broken and as v. 17 in the Amplified Bible says, they "humbly seek forgiveness." The tax gatherer in Luke 18 would be an example of the third category.

So, attempting to stick the "everybody plays broken" thought into the context of your marriage, if you believe you are married to a "bad" wife and are in a "bad" marriage, there is every likelihood you're either in category one or two and are seriously playing broken but are either too arrogant to admit your own brokenness or so broken you can't see how broken you are. This last possibility is a nasty one. This kind of marital brokenness is the one that sees logs in her eyes and, at best, sawdust in their own (Luke 18).

So, what's a boy to do with all this brokenness? There's a couple possibilities. First, God can be massively glorified through our exchanged-life, broken relating. What I mean by this is, as you, in your brokenness, continue to work at loving your "bad" wife in your broken ways, God gets glorified (seen as loving, wise, and powerful, as He is). Why? Because you are so messed up; so opposite of her; having nothing in common with her; and are so seriously selfish and self-centered, that as you rest in and rely on Him to love your "bad" wife through you, you, your "bad" wife, and the rest of the world recognize that the only way this kind of love is possible is that there must be a God out there somewhere making it happen (John 13:35).

Secondly, healing takes place. What I mean by healing is, when two broken people experience God's unconditional love and acceptance (grace), they heal and become less broken, God's love, forgiveness, and acceptance fill, as it were, the "broken" cracks in us and we heal. As God is making you less broken, you now have something to give. Remembering that you can't give what you don't have, not even to yourself; the healing you received from Him can now be passed on to her. That healing can look something like, "I know that you're broken. I know what you did really hurt me. I forgive and love you anyway." As we focus on the reality that we are massively broken and still loved, forgiven, and accepted by God, we are able, in our brokenness and in His power, to pass that same love, forgiveness, and acceptance on to our "bad" wife.

God's unconditional love, forgiveness, and acceptance, passed on to her through God's grace (His power and desire, miraculously working through us), can undo the brokenness that everyone plays with.

It's not perfect. But God created it for His glory and our good. This is the only opportunity we have to experience it. With God's help, why not make the most of it?

Genesis 2:22; Matthew 22:30;
1 Corinthians 13:10; Galatians 2:20

An Imperfect Marriage Is Perfectly OK

Performers are one of the "sick," "broken" types I wrote about in the last section, who think they're healthy and everyone else is sick. A performer would be the equivalent of the New Testament Pharisee, such as Simon in Luke 7. One of the problems with performers is that they look good. Not only do they look good, but they usually are "good," at least on the outside while others are looking (Matt 6:5).

With a performer, how things look is always more important than how things are (Matt 23:27). Since they look so externally good, they're usually pretty intimidating. One of the ways they're intimidating is they have a tendency to compare their perceived strengths, with the obvious, observable sins and weaknesses of others. And because they look so good on the outside, they have, at least in their mind, earned the "right" to identify and point out the faults of others. The sad reality about the performer's finger-pointing is, again, they're usually right ("she's a sinner," Luke 7:39).

Like Simon, performers have very accurate observations, but really bad conclusions. The performer's conclusions always end in law, never grace. Grace doesn't fit their narrative. Pharisees and performers are allergic to grace. Why? Because everyone wins when grace is applied. As we saw earlier, everyone's sick, everyone's broken, everyone needs grace. The problem is, with the performer, there has to be a winner and it really needs to be them. Grace on the other hand has very different conclusions; "the first shall be last in the last shall be first" (Matt 19:30). Grace-rules don't compute for the performer.

Here's a little secret about the performer, they can't keep the rules either. They look like they can because they work so hard while others are looking. But performers have a shadow life. They have a behind-the-scenes life. They look good while the spotlight is on them, but they have an amazing tendency to look for, find, and live in the shadows, away from the spotlights. The shadows are where the performer goes to do their dirty deeds; where hopefully those who matter won't be, and will never see. They are the performers who perform for audiences, but backstage, when the curtain is drawn, are struggling just like the rest of us.

If you've ever lived with a performer, you'll recognize this next character trait. Performers never forgive. They are professional resentments keepers. One of the reasons they never forgive is because it keeps them in the "I'm always right" position. You may have done 99.99 percent of it right, but they will look at and accurately identify the .01% you did wrong. They will not only accurately identify and point out your fault but keep pointing it out whenever that little shame-filled trump card is needed to win a future disagreement.

This section was pretty easy for me to write. The reason for the ease is because I'm a performer. I come from a long, long line of professional performers and resentment keepers. All these sins, character flaws, and more apply to me and my biological family. These characteristics are fairly easy to put on paper. I just look at me and my family, and type. Now I'm obviously not proud of this. Little by little, God is identifying these sin-filled character flaws in me and I'm grateful. Laurie is especially grateful. She's been graciously living with this obnoxious performer for nearly thirty years now. Thanks, Laurie.

But why all the hubbub about performers in a section that was supposed to be about imperfection being perfectly okay? Because as we saw in the previous section, performers are massively sick and broken, they just don't see it.

One of the reasons the performer gene is so damaging in marriage is because the performer actually believes he's doing God a favor when pointing out the .01 percent faults in others (Luke 18:9–14). It is nearly impossible to try to get him to see that he's actually distancing himself from his "bad" wife with his persistent faultfindings. The finger-pointing is not helpful or healing. The "bad" wife may actually be in the process of, figuratively speaking, drying her tears from Jesus' feet with her hair (Luke 7:36–38), but sadly, the performer is more focused on how embarrassing this humiliating display is, than that his "bad" wife is experiencing forgiveness and spiritual healing.

Here's a sad insight in regard to the performer's "bad" wife experiencing God's grace. Grace gives energy, faultfinding crushes it. As your "bad" wife is experiencing God's grace, she will begin to look more like Jesus in her thoughts, attitudes, and behaviors. The only problem is that no matter how well she "performs," it will never be good enough in the eyes of the performer. In Jesus' eyes she was always loved and accepted in the middle of her "bad" performance. But in the eyes of her performer husband (you and me) she will never be good enough. Even if your "bad" wife is "performing" well today, her perceived flaws and imperfections from her past will continue to be the relational lens you use to taint and tarnish whatever good she may have done or is currently doing.

So again, even if she's doing her best, it will never measure up and you will continue to see her as a "bad" wife in a "bad" marriage. Literarily with the performer, she can never win. Your sinful drive to have a perfect marriage is going to suck the life out of your "bad" wife and your "bad" marriage.

One of the ways to deal with your sin of being a performer is to realize that Jesus' performance for you on the cross was enough. "It is finished." He performed so you and she don't have to. Next, place on the altar of God, as a sacrifice to Him, your sinful need to be perfect. Say something like, "God, I place my drive for perfection on Your alter. I give it up and accept Your free gift of grace and enoughness" (Rom 5:1; Eph 2:8–9; Col 1:22).

Next I will, as a matter of my will (not my emotions) pass Your love, forgiveness, and acceptance on to my "bad" wife. You may have to do this on a daily, even hourly basis as the ugly performance drive continues to pop its performance-oriented head up. I do not believe that you will be able to get rid of this ungodly drive on your own. Jesus will have to do this through you.

Just Love Her

Yes, whomever the performer is married to, is going to have many .01 percent faults. The cool thing is that as she is learning about, and in Jesus' name experiencing, His love, forgiveness, and acceptance, even if the performing husband doesn't get it, the imperfect, "bad" wife, in her imperfect, "bad" ways of relating, in Jesus' name is perfectly okay. God's grace covers it even if the performing husband doesn't.

"Now to the *performer*, his wages are not credited as a favor or a gift, but as an obligation [something owed to him]. But to the one who does not *perform* [that is, the one who does not try to earn his *ok-ness through self-performance*] but believes and completely trusts in Him who justifies the ungodly, his faith is credited to him as righteousness [right standing with God]" (paraphrased from Rom 4:4–5 Amplified Bible, italics mine).

An imperfect marriage is perfectly OK.

She didn't mean it for evil, but You meant it for good.

Genesis 50:20

If He Were My Number One Passion, She Wouldn't Be My Number One Problem

Has something or someone besides Jesus become your number one passion? Being more specific, has your "bad" wife become the number one passion of your life?

You might ask, "Well, how would I know?" Here are a few indicators:

You dwell on (functional worship) her characteristics (good or "bad") more frequently than His.

You say yes to her and no to God when it should have been the other way around.

Her touch brings more joy than His (1 Sam 10:26).

"Distance" from her hurts more than distance from Him.

It hurts more to hear "no" from her than Him.

You run to her instead of Him as your primary need-meeter.

It's easier to spend "your" time and money on her than Him.

You get mad at Him for something she did or didn't do.

You get mad at Him because she didn't turn out like you planned.

You've had thoughts that said, "Life isn't worth living," when she or your marriage turned "bad."

I'm sure there are many other indicators, but the problem comes when we attempt to get from our "bad" wives what only God can give. We do this all the time and there's a very high likelihood this is one of the reasons you're reading this little book, but may not have put all the pieces together yet.

Why do we do this? Because it works. At least for a while. In the beginning, while she is still unknown and everything is new and exciting, she "works." We believe and feel as if being with, getting to know, and enjoying her is meeting so many of our previously unmet needs for love, acceptance, power, and success that weren't being met, though our relationship with Jesus (our problem not His). The problem with healthy love is, it's so easily derailed. The derailment comes when we run to her before or instead of God to meet our God-shaped-vacuum needs (2 Cor 11:3).

Why do we do this? Is there a possibility that for years we have walked around with at least two things running around inside of us? First is a "God-shaped vacuum" (Pascal). Second is a fantasized version of the perfect woman that's going to fill that "God-shaped vacuum." When we eventually meet our fantasized, female-vacuum-filler, we, at least initially, are able to check off a lot of the previously unchecked vacuum-filled boxes. We think, "Dang! She's amazing!" I no longer feel empty. I no longer feel full of vacuum. But here's where the potential of derailment in our healthy love for her and God comes in. Because she's right here, has skin, and is easily accessible, we run to her instead of Him as our primary vacuum-filler.

I don't think that most of us do this in an evil, anti-first-commandment way (Exod 20:3). At the time, we're more into "it's not good for man to be alone" than "have no other gods before me." But when being with her erases so many of our long-experienced lonelinesses and vacuums, we start to mentally say, "If a little is good, then a lot's got to be better." At this point she becomes the "cat's meow." We are getting that God-shaped vacuum "filled," with something other than God, with an intensity we never thought possible, on a timetable that we have some level of control over, and darn it, this feels really good! Kind of like how I've always wanted to feel on my terms and my timetable. We then, most of the time unwittingly, take this beautiful gift from Jesus, our wives, and make an idol out of 'em (Ezek 16:15–19). She has now become our number one passion and a "bad" wife.

Here's a problem with other-than-God, number-one-passion idols, whenever I make a second-place thing first, I have neither. What I mean by this is any time I take anything and put it in God's first place, that second-place thing blows up. No person, place, position, possession, or thing can be in God's first-place slot. And no person, place, position, possession, or thing can handle the pressure of being in God's first-place slot. Only God can handle that position. I will also create a sense of distance, on my part, not His, during this time of messed-up passions and positionings and as a by-product, I may find it difficult or feel uneasy to return to my true first-place-passion, Jesus.

If it helps, think about the difficulty the prodigal son had when he was thinking about returning to his father after having made prostitutes and partying his number one passion (Luke 15:17–19). God many times allows us, for a period of time, to have messed-up passions. He then eventually takes away that second-place thing I placed in His slot. He loves me too much to allow my self-appointed counterfeits to steal the true joy that He wants me to enjoy (Ps 16). Like the prodigal, there's usually some hard times involved to get me/us to turn back to resting in and relying on Him as our number-one-slot-passion-filler.

So how does God take away our idols? He designs situations that expose the weaknesses in and the inabilities of our second-place idols to fill our God-shaped-vacuum needs. He lovingly handcrafts horrible situations that expose our idols to be as inadequate and impotent as they truly are. There's a good possibility that's one of the reasons you're reading this little book. God may be in the process of exposing the weaknesses and inabilities of your second-place idol, your "bad" wife, of residing in his first-place-position as you're reading this.

I want to try to say this again, God is in the process of exposing the reality that you have made an idol out of your "bad" wife and the way He's doing it is through the pain you're experiencing from not getting your God-only vacuum needs met through your "bad" wife.

There's a wonderful illustration of this in 2 Sam 5:20–21, where the Philistines on a couple of occasions attempted to fight the Israelites and failed. After the second failure, the passage says that "the Philistines abandoned their idols there." Why did they do this? Because their idols didn't work. We do the same thing with the idols we have created of our "bad" wives. We are angry at our wives because God is designing relational battles we cannot win, in order to force us to "abandon" our "bad-wife" idols.

If Jesus were our number-one-passion, if we were running to Him instead of her, we wouldn't be relationally dissatisfied and/or empty because she's not our number-one-need-meeter—*He* is. We wouldn't be overwhelmed with that void because it wouldn't be there. Why? Because our God-shaper-vacuum-filler would be in His rightful, number-one-passion-filler-place, not our "bad" wife.

As the old hymn goes, "Turn your eyes upon Jesus. Look full in His wonderful face. And the things of earth will grow strangely dim. In the light of His glory and grace."[5]

If He were my number-one-passion, she wouldn't be my number one problem.

---

5. Helen H. Lemmel, "Turn Your Eyes upon Jesus," 1922.

God puts us through stuff so that when others tell us their stuff, we don't blink.

2 Corinthians 1:2–7

Love Him When You "Can't" Love Her

"The person who has My commandments and keeps them is the one who [really] loves Me; and whoever [really] loves Me will be loved by My Father, and I will love him and reveal Myself to him [I will make Myself real to him]" (John 14:21 Amplified Bible).

"Love is patient, love is kind, it is not jealous; love does not brag, it is not arrogant. It does not act disgracefully, it does not seek its own benefit; it is not provoked, does not keep an account of a wrong suffered, it does not rejoice in unrighteousness, but rejoices with the truth; it keeps every confidence, it believes all things, hopes all things, endures all things" (1 Cor 13:4-7 NASB).

There will be times when I can't stand my "bad" wife. This is my sin not hers. The thought of being kind and dropping my self-centeredness (1 Cor 13:4-5) is simply out of the question. In those times where I "can't" (most likely won't) love her, *love Him.*

How? First, I focus on how He has unconditionally loved and forgiven me over all these years of sin and idolatries ("chief of sinners," 1 Tim 1:15). Next, I take seriously John 14:21 and remember how much I love Him, because He first loved me (1 John 4:19), and in His power and living His exchanged life through me, I surrender to, depend on, trust in, and obey what He said in 1 Cor 13:4-5—and *voila!* I just told Jesus I love Him by doing what He told me to do for my wife, in His power.

I don't necessarily need to tell my wife the process that just took place. But as I continue this process of loving Him when I "can't" love her, there's a good chance that Jesus will energize my heart due to my investing what's important to me (time, money, effort, her love language, and many times just keeping my mouth shut) into what was initially impossible (Luke 12:34).

Just Love Her

That's how to love Him, when you "can't" love her.

Just because my life feels like hell, doesn't mean it's her job to make it feel like heaven.

1 Peter 4:19

Turbocharging the Love-Him-When-You-"Can't"-Love-Her Thing

"Although He was a Son [who had never been disobedient to the Father], He learned [active, special] obedience through what He suffered" (Heb 5:8 Amplified Bible).

OK, new scenario: You're in the I-"can't"-love-her thing again. But this time it's because she did something that hurt you and caused you pain, suffering, hardship, disappointment, sadness, etc. This is going to be really hard because what she did or didn't do really hurt, a lot. But Jesus and the Bible said to love and keep forgiving her even when she hurts you, really badly (Eph 5:25; Matt 18:21–22).

Again, just like in the last section, remind yourself that you can't give what you don't have. Next, remind yourself how much He has loved and forgiven you. Now that you've reminded yourself (keep doing it if necessary), even though you feel empty, angry, or resentful, you now choose to focus on how full of love and forgiveness He is and has been toward you, and, based on the reality that Jesus died on the cross for you (Rom 3:23–24), and that God loves you as much as He loves Jesus (John 17:23), you now have, in His power, His love and forgiveness to give her.

The turbocharging part of this suffering-infused scenario with your "bad" wife is to consider that Jesus "learned obedience from the things He suffered" (Heb 5:8). Obviously we know that Jesus never sinned (2 Cor 5:21; Heb 4:15). His "learning" doesn't mean He was a disobedient youngster and grew into an obedient adult. It's more like Jesus increased in His submission, surrendering, and obedience to God as His God-directed sufferings increased. The ultimate example of this was when Jesus in the garden said,

Just Love Her

"Father, if you are willing, please take this cup of suffering away from Me. Yet I want Your will to be done, not Mine" (Luke 22:42).

God-directed sufferings give us the opportunity to grow in our obedience to Him. We need to look at our current pain and suffering as an opportunity to not only evidence our love for Him (John 14:21), but also see this as an opportunity to supercharge Jesus' promise of my getting to more intimately know Him (John 14:21; Phil 1:29; 3:10).

I'm going to try to keep this simple and just throw out some thoughts for both my and hopefully your benefit. So, when I obey:

1. It evidences my love for Jesus (John 14:21).
2. God and Jesus will love me (John 14:21). Now this is a little weird. Jesus and God never increase or decrease their love for me based on what I do or don't do. Their love for me/us is consistent based on who They are and that They've chosen to love me/us (Ps 59:10; 1 John 4:10; Titus 3:5). So, this portion of 14:21 is not talking about God increasing His love for us, but rather us getting a clearer, more consistent experience of His love, without the distractions of guilt and shame, sin and rebellion on my part (Gen 2:25).
3. Jesus says that as we obey, He will more intimately "reveal" Himself to us. In the same way Moses, Elijah, Hosea, and Paul wanted to know Him, He will do His "revealing" for us (Exod 33:12–23; 2 Kgs 6:17–20; Hos 6:6; Phil 3:8).
4. When I obey in the context of suffering, it somehow supercharges the first three benefits. "He learned [active, special] obedience through what He suffered."
5. As I am receiving, resting in, and experiencing these three benefits of my dependent obedience to God in the middle of pain-filled relational sorrow, I now have His love, forgiveness, and acceptance to give to my "bad" wife, even if I don't feel like it. That's how to turbocharge my love toward Him and her, when I "can't" love her.

One way to get rid of resentments I may have toward my "bad" wife is to remember that *the sins I can't forget about her are the sins He chooses not to remember about me and her.* I'm hanging on to junk about my wife that God chose to forget before she ever sinned. His grace gives me the ability to love and forgive her in the same way He already loves and forgave me . . . and her.

1 John 4:12; Hebrews 8:12

Placing the Truth of God over Emotions

"Anyone who intends to come with Me has to let Me lead. You're not in the driver's seat; I am. Don't run from suffering; embrace it. Follow Me and I'll show you how" (Matt 16:25 *The Message*).

This Matthew 16 passage has been driving me crazy. I know it's massively important in regard to letting go of my perception of my "bad" marriage and embracing the truth that she is my "perfect gift" (Jas 1:17) from Jesus and the "whom God has put together" woman for me. But when I'm in the middle of my "bad" marriage and I'm confused, angry, scared, or panic-stricken, those truths and the process I'm gonna talk about are really hard.

The reason it's hard is that I place too much faith in my feelings. I can literally be reading this Matthew 16 passage or similar passages that tell me how much He loves me, or verses that say He's in charge, and at the same time, because my emotions are screaming, and the verses I'm reading are only whispering, the verses end up sounding like the adults in all the *Charlie Brown* TV cartoons, blah, blah, blah, blah, blah, blah, blah.

There have been times when my emotions come across as having the authoritative power of God's voice from the clouds (Matt 3:17). I can be reading encouraging and powerful verses from the Bible and at the same time hear myself telling myself, "They're just words." I know this is wrong and messed up, but it's true at times.

In daily practice, if and when this happens, I'm going to have to bypass or sidestep my emotions and make a volitional choice, whether I feel like it or not, to say, "Even if I don't feel it, Jesus, I know Your words are true and I choose to trust and believe You and what You've said more than my emotions."

I'm gonna take a sidestep for a second and get a little more specific on how to actually set your emotion aside. Our emotions are a direct by-product of our predominant thought. I define predominant as my current or repeated thought. If I'm constantly thinking about how someone lied to me in the past, I may have the accompanying feelings of sadness, anger, resentment, or fear. If on the other hand I choose to have predominant thoughts of worship, of mentally looking at the character of God and who He is, I will as Psalm 16 says, experience "joy" and "pleasure" instead of the other negative emotions. So, one of the ways we can set our emotions aside is to change our predominant thought (2 Cor 10:5; Ps 119:9, 11).

Joshua 1:6–9 gives another example of placing our intellect over our emotions. It says, "Be strong and courageous, for you are the one who will lead these people to possess all the land I swore to their ancestors I would give them. Be strong and very courageous. Be careful to obey all the instructions Moses gave you. Do not deviate from them, turning either to the right or to the left. Then you will be successful in everything you do. Study this Book of Instruction continually. Meditate on it day and night so you will be sure to obey everything written in it. Only then will you prosper and succeed in all you do. This is My command—be strong and courageous! Do not be afraid or discouraged. For the Lord your God is with you wherever you go." These were the predominant thoughts God gave Joshua to think and dwell on.

We'll want to develop the discipline of dependence, through His power, of letting the truths of the Bible rule over our emotions. Most of what God tells us to do makes sense and most of us already know the right thing to believe, trust, and do. The problem comes when we choose to ruminate on, trust in, and make a priority of our feelings over what God has told us to do and what He said is true (Josh 1:6–9). What He's telling us is to study, meditate, and obey His word(s).

So, the "Book of Instruction" and the truths of God that we're going to attempt to be "sure to obey" are what we'll want to place over or allow to rule our emotions.

So, getting back to the Matthew 16 passage, one goal might be to make predominant thoughts out of the truths from this passage. This could look something like:

- In and through Your strength and power I want to follow You, Jesus.
- Jesus, You're in charge, I'm not.
- In Your strength and in Your power, Jesus, I won't run from suffering but embrace it.
- Jesus, You will show me how to embrace the suffering I'm currently involved in.

So, when in the context of my "bad" marriage, I begin to experience various forms of suffering, I will choose, in His power, to create predominant thoughts based on Bible passages like Matthew 16:25, and instead of running from the suffering, I will choose to embrace it. Relying on Jesus' help, the truthfulness of the Bible and the exchanged-life discipline of truth-filled, predominant thoughts, I will embrace the suffering that Jesus has designed for my life and continue to follow Him. That's how to let the truths of God rule over emotions.

If the driver's seat of who I am (my heart) is occupied by a driver who has been misled by my deceptive heart, what makes me think that I am the best judge of what my "bad" wife and "bad" marriage should look like?

Jeremiah 17:9

Dipping Toes and Letting Goes

So, let's see if we can get a little more practical in regard to the last section focusing on Jesus' directive of embracing suffering. I want to look at another passage that might make it easier to rest in and depend on Jesus for this thing of setting aside our emotions in the face of "sufferings."

There's this amazing, set-your-emotions-aside story in Joshua 3. The story actually begins in chapter 1, where God, speaking to Joshua, says, "Moses my servant is dead. Therefore, the time has come for you to lead these people, the Israelites, across the Jordan River into the land I am giving them." The "suffering" that Joshua and the Israelites were going to face consisted of two impossible challenges. The first challenge they needed to overcome was to cross what was previously thought to be uncrossable, the Jordan River. The second impossible challenge they had to "suffer" was to attack and conquer what was previously thought to be unconquerable, the city of Jericho. I want to focus on the first challenge of crossing the Jordan.

Now I know there's lots of details that I could get into, but I'm not going to. Keeping it simple, it was a scary and dangerous thing for a group of people to think about crossing a river the size of the Jordan. It was literally impossible, that's why God had to get involved. Crossing the Jordan was a dangerous proposal, a form of suffering that they were going to have to embrace because God told them to do it.

So, God, in 3:13 says, "As soon as their (the priests) feet touch the water, the flow of water will be cut off upstream, and the river will stand up like a wall." "As soon their feet touch the water." Why couldn't the flow of water have stopped a couple of days before they were supposed to cross the Jordan? That would've been nice and far less scary. But for the most part, God doesn't work that way. He tells us what to do, then He does it through us. But for the most part, we don't get to see or feel that He's doing it until we, in faith, step out and do it. Then "the flow of water will be cut off" in the challenges He's directed us to overcome.

So, here's the point of this section. As they were walking up to this raging river, fear and emotions raging as well, they were going to have to set their emotions aside, trust in what God said and promised, embrace their "suffering" and stick their big toe in the water. And you know the rest of the story. Big toes go in, impossible challenge goes out.

Putting this Joshua 3 and the Matthew 16 passages together in the context of our "bad" marriages, we're going to have to walk up to and face the "suffering(s)" in our "bad" marriages and mentally and spiritually stick our big toes in those scary relational waters and then watch for the miracle. The practical way of "sticking our toes in" is to continue to *just love her* and develop true-truth predominant thoughts such as:

1. I want to follow Jesus, even if my "bad" marriage is killing me right now.
2. You're in charge of me and my "bad" marriage, not me.
3. With Your help, I won't run from the suffering I'm currently experiencing in my "bad" marriage but will face it in Your power.
4. Jesus, You will show me how to face the suffering I'm currently experiencing in my "bad" marriage (Jas 1:5).

One of the primary ways to stay the course, "embrace the suffering," and continue to *just love her*, is to mentally set aside our emotions, believe what Jesus in the Bible says, and in His power, stick your relational big toe in the Jordan of your "bad" marriage, and watch God do His thing. That's dipping toes and letting goes!

Is there a possibility the reason God said "good and not evil" in this verse was because He wanted to remind us of the truth in the middle of difficult times? That even if it feels bad and evil, it's not.

I wonder if Jeremiah 29:11 could apply to our "bad" marriages?

With a Significant *Why*, We (He and I) Can Handle Any *What*

(Consider the relational iceberg when thinking about this section.)

The *what* of this little thought is focused on our "bad" marriage. The "you," in this case is addressed to Christians, and as a by-product includes Jesus working through us (Rom 5:10; Gal 2:20). And finally, the *why* pretty obviously speaks to our motivation which in this case is to first reconnect with our First and primary love affair, Jesus. The second would be to hope that by allowing Jesus to be our number one love, we would *just love her*, rather than make an idol out of her.

So, why did you get married? Personal fulfillment? Relational satisfaction? Legitimate sex? Little or no self-control (1 Cor 7:9)? Overwhelming loneliness? There are many motivations or *whys* for getting married. Whatever it/they were, your *why* for staying married will most likely need to change.

One of the first reasons you'll need to change *whys* in order to stay married is that no matter how much you thought you knew her, you didn't. It doesn't matter if you were "childhood sweethearts" or a "love at first sight" couple, you didn't know the, what I'm going to call the 24/7 person. When you're married to someone it's impossible to hide the things you either consciously or unconsciously hid when being seen only part time, such as on a date or at school. When you begin to see the real, 24/7 person, for the first time, it's kinda scary. You may begin to think, "Who the heck are you?" Or that you were either tricked, lied to, or manipulated into marriage. The other problem is there's a high likelihood you'll begin to blame her for not being "as advertised."

Another reason you'll need to change *whys* is because you're changing. It's impossible for two people to live in daily, close proximity for any length of time and go unchanged. As that famous marital expert Sir Isaac Newton said, "An object in motion tends to stay in motion unless an external force acts upon it." The two of you are "external forces" that "act" upon each other, hopefully "until death do us part." Messing with Newton's thought from a marital counseling perspective, "you can't stay the same in marriage." To put it another way, my wife, Laurie, has slept with at least five different men in the almost thirty years I've known her. All five of them were me.

Marriage is like a rock tumbler. You and I are the equivalent of sharp-edged, unattractive, difficult-to-live-with rocks. God places us in the tumbler of marriage, and we change. The difficulties, challenges, losses, and disappointments of our handcrafted, God-ordained pain of this God-designed tumbler of marriage changes us. Because of this relational tumbling, my *why* to stay married is going to have to change.

Another change agent in marriage is insight. Now that you're actually doing marriage rather than just reading about it, the time in and pains of marriage change you. Unless you found a way to live under a relational rock while married, you're going to gain insight and understanding. The insight and understanding change you, as long as you surrender and allow the humbling (tumbling) process to do its thing.

Let me give a simple example from the game of chess. If you play both sides of a chess board, alone, with no competition, you always win. You're always "right." But, with another player, there's now the possibility you can lose and be "wrong." The losing and not always being "right" are humbling, and as you "keep playing the game," you'll end up learning and hopefully applying new insights and understandings of how to improve your "play," and as a by-product, stay in the game of marriage and relating.

Paul in 1 Corinthians 7 uses the entire chapter to promote a number of *whys* for staying single. And obviously because it's in the Bible, I agree with what God and Paul are saying (2 Tim 3:16). At the same time, if you're like me and already married, the *whys* of staying single aren't necessarily helpful.

I however want to use Paul's instructions from chapter 7, specifically from v. 34 as a biblically inspired *why* to stay married. Verse 34 says that a married man's "interests are divided," and as a by-product he will find it more difficult to be completely devoted to Jesus due to the added distractions of trying to please both God and his "bad" wife simultaneously.

Since we married guys have "divided interests," we'll have the opportunity to get to know Jesus and be devoted to Him in ways no single person ever could. We're going to have to spin more marital, parental, professional, and spiritual plates due to our need and desire to please both Jesus and our "bad" wives. With Jesus living His supernatural life in and through us, we now have a powerful, passion-filled *why* for being and staying married (Ezek 36:26).

So, one of your and my *whys* can be the same as Paul's, Hosea's, and the guys who wrote the West Minister Shorter Catechism, that of knowing and glorifying Jesus. Based on what we talked about earlier and from what God has been showing you in your Bible reading and life experience, you already believe and are resting in the reality that God wanted you married, not single. Why? Because you're married, not single. So, the new *why* of being and staying married is to first know, glorify, and serve Jesus better while married. Next would be, as a by-product of your knowing Him better, you will love and serve your "bad" wife better, and as another by-product, God will be glorified by your new *why* of being and staying married. Here's a few verses to consider:

- "So whether you eat or drink, or whatever you do, do it all for the glory of God" (1 Cor 10:31).
- "I want you to show love, not offer sacrifices. I want you to know Me more than I want burnt offerings" (Hos 6:6).

- "Everything else is worthless when compared with the infinite value of knowing Christ Jesus my Lord . . . I want to know Christ . . ." (Phil 3:8, 10).
- "The married man's primary *why* is to glorify God, and to enjoy Him forever" while married (paraphrase of the Westminster Shorter Catechism).

Now at this point, I want to remind you of the "you can't do this" section at the beginning of this book. This wasn't easy to write, and it certainly isn't easy to live out. Actually, it's impossible. The only way this section is going to take place in your marriage is if Jesus is your number one passion and you surrender and get out of the way and let Him live His life of love through you to her. The only way I know to make that happen is to, on a daily basis, ask God to take away all your idols and make Himself your number one passion. This is a prayer He loves and will answer.

With a significant *why*, we (He and I) can handle any *what*.

He separated Himself from the love of His life in order to be restored to the loves of His life.

Hebrews 12:2

What's Impossible for Me Is a Walk in the Park for Him

There's this wonderful story in Matthew 14 that's a perfect illustration of how we so many times get overwhelmed and in a panic over our "bad" wives in our "bad" marriages. The objective truth of our overwhelmedness, is that Jesus is right in the middle of our panic, taking a casual walk in our relational park. My goal here is to show that during those times we think all is lost and there's no hope for our "bad" marriages, there is. What's currently scaring us to death in our "bad" marriage, is something that Jesus is lovingly, sovereignly, compassionately not only in charge of, but has designed, not just allowed.

In the Matthew 14 account, Jesus has just concluded one of His most amazing miracles by feeding five thousand people with little more than a Happy Meal. Jesus then moves on to set up this chapter 14 scenario. I want to say this again, Jesus set up this scenario. It didn't just happen, and He didn't just allow it. He is handcrafting another opportunity, right on the heels of His miraculously catered meal, to demonstrate to the disciples that He is trustworthy and capable in the middle of impossible situations.

Verse 22 reads, "Jesus insisted that His disciples get back into the boat and cross to the other side of the lake," while He stayed there and said goodbye to the people He just fed. Soon after the disciples left, the passage says that the "disciples were in trouble." Again, Jesus set this up. This wasn't an accident. This wasn't an oops-moment. Jesus did this. He handcrafted this impossibly out-of-control situation, in an environment that most of the men in the boat would have normally felt pretty comfortable in and familiar with.

Just Love Her

Remember, many of the men in the boat were fishermen. What normally would have been a walk in the park for them was now an impossibly out-of-control, panic-stricken wreck of the Edmund Fitzgerald moment. The Bible says they were "far away from land," they were struggling with "strong winds" and "big waves," and it was "late at night." The disciples were panicking. This was "bad."

In the middle of the disciple's out-of-controllness, Jesus comes walking on the water. What seemed impossible for the disciples was a walk in the park for Jesus. In an environment the disciples knew like the back of their proverbial fishermen's hands, was now a Jesus-designed, impossibly out-of-control situation. Why? Because that's what He does (Phil 1:29). He handcrafts horrible situations for our good and His glory. Impossibly out-of-control situations just like the one you're currently in, in your "bad" marriage.

As an interesting side note, in v. 26, when Jesus first started approaching them in order to help, they thought He was a ghost. They didn't recognize Him. This will be true of us as well when we're in the middle of our relational panic. There's every likelihood that the overwhelmednesses we'll be experiencing while in our relational-panic mode will make it difficult for us to "see" Him while He's walking toward us in our storm. And many times, even when we see Jesus walking on our relational waters to help, we'll blame Him for the "big waves," rather than get on our knees and thank Him for coming to our rescue.

The mental picture I get of this scenario in the context of our "bad" marriages looks like this: It's late at night / early morning. Always a scary time. It's dark and confusing, a perfect time to panic.

I can't see the shore: no security. I can't see my past—those times when Jesus came to my rescue before. Or worse, my brain has a tendency to remember just the nasty stuff from my past, the stuff that hurt, the stuff that disappointed. Again, scary time. Perfect time to panic.

Just Love Her

I can't see a lighthouse: No future. No hope. It's real easy to see the difficulties, the overwhelmingnesses, the hopelessnesses of my "bad" marriage, in this perfectly designed time to panic.

I can see the big waves. I can feel the wind: in the middle of my panic, but initially, I can't see Jesus walking on the water to come and help. Perfect time to panic.

In my mind, this is impossibly out of control. Perfect time to panic.

What's a panic-stricken boy to do? First off, focus on who He is, how He's always come through in the past, and what He's promised for our future. Remember, in the middle of fear and panic, we place too much faith in our feelings. Feelings scream. God's truth and the Holy Spirit whisper. We have to, with God's help, surrender to the need of setting our emotions aside and believing what Jesus says here. "Don't be afraid. Take courage. I am here."

When it's late at night / early in the morning and really dark (relationally speaking): "Don't be afraid. Take courage. I am here."

When I can't see the shore; when I see my past pessimistically (relationally speaking): "Don't be afraid. Take courage. I am here."

When I can't see a lighthouse; when I see no hope for my future (relationally speaking): "Don't be afraid. Take courage. I am here."

When I'm in a relational-panic, and all I can see is the terrifying relational waves, and feel the terrifying relational wind and all hope is gone: "Don't be afraid. Take courage. I am here."

When I believe my "bad" marriage is impossibly out of control and lost: "Don't be afraid. Take courage. I am here."

Remember, in the same way Jesus designed this situation for His glory and the disciple's good, He designed that you two be together. Your jaunt across this wind- and wave-infested relational lake of marriage was planned by Jesus. Remember, He knew in advance, He planned those relational waves. He planned these nasty relational winds. Your "bad" marriage isn't an accident. It's not a mistake. What you see as an impossibly out-of-control marital situation is a walk in the park for Him.

You are the Love of my life. She is my wife.
If you want to be my follower you must love Me
more than your wife.

Luke 14:26

Which Is a Bigger Deal, That You Get Satisfied or That God Gets Glorified?

I once heard some Christian "expert" say something like, "There are certain couples in bad marriages that continue to struggle through them, as if God can't tell the difference between a good and bad marriage, just because a piece of paper is still signed." I'm going to hope and believe that when he made this statement about God's observations of good and bad marriages, he was attempting to expose certain legalistic, how-things-look-is-more-important-than-how-things-are, Pharisaical, performance-oriented marriages. It seemed as if he might have been trying to say that God wants us to "live in peace" in our marriages (1 Cor 7:15). And if the couple had done all they could, expired all options, and it's still a "bad" marriage, it might be time to unsign the paper.

If unsigning was what he was suggesting, I would like to politely disagree. I want to promote the value of struggling in and through "bad" marriages. Obviously, God can tell the difference between good and bad marriages. But is a "good" marriage God's highest priority in marriage? I wonder if the more important priority, from God's perspective, is not my having a pain-free, uber-satisfying, "good" marriage, but a marriage that glorifies Him?

Another question that might be asked is, "Can God be glorified through a 'bad' marriage?"

Before I go any further, I'd like to give my simple definition of what glorifying God is. Very simply, God gets glorified when He gets seen as good as He is. That's it. And in regard to His getting seen as good as He is, there's bonus points when we go through His handcrafted, impossible-without-Him, out-of-control situations, in His power, with the motivation of His being seen as good as He is, as He helps us through it. Besides glorifying Him, we will get to know Him better and grow stronger in our ability to stick it out in the next hard time (John 14:21; Rom 5:3–5; 2 Cor 1:4–11).

An example of this is found in John 9. In this story Jesus and his disciples meet a man who was "born blind." I'm not going to go into a lot of the details of this passage, but what I will do is focus on why Jesus said this man was born blind. He said, "This happened so the power of God could be seen in him." More simply, this very "bad" situation was handcrafted by God so that He could be seen as good as He is by healing this man's blindness. That's how God gets glorified.

Let's jump in a little deeper. Back in the book of Exodus, God is talking to Moses, and He says in 4:11, "Who gave human beings their mouths? Who makes them deaf or mute? Who gives them sight or makes them blind? Is it not I, the Lord?" In this passage we see that God admits that when a person is born deaf, mute, or in the case of this man in John 9, blind, God is the one who did it. This is really hard for many Christians to wrap their brains around (me included). They soften difficult scenarios by saying "God allowed it." No, based on this passage God Himself takes credit for designing and determining what challenges people are born with and will struggle with during their lives. So, in the context of this John 9 scenario, we know that this man was born blind, God made him blind and He did it for His glory.

There's a real hiccup here. If you hooked up with Jesus for the main purpose of Him making your life more successful, more comfortable, more satisfying, you're gonna have a real problem with God doing something as painful as purposefully having a man born blind so that He could be seen as cool as He is. That's the problem. Many of us, me included, are more into God glorifying our lives than we are in us glorifying His.

Is there a possibility that this interaction between Jesus and this blind man could be applied to our "bad" marriage? If we were to look at the passage again, when the disciples found out that the man was blind, the first thing they did was try to place blame. They asked if it was the man or his parents who sinned that caused the man's blindness. Jesus said no, you're asking the wrong question. The real priority here is that God gets seen as good as He is in the middle of impossibly "bad" situations.

Is there a possibility that you have been asking the wrong question and placing blame wrongfully on your "bad" wife for your "bad" marriage? Is there a possibility (and I think there is), that your "bad" marriage was predetermined by God? Understanding that neither of you are to blame, but that "this marriage took place so the power of God could be seen in your 'bad' marriage" (paraphrased from v. 3)? Is there a possibility that God is more interested in being glorified through your pain, suffering (Phil 1:29; 1 Pet 4:19), and efforts, in His power to not just live in, but glorify Him in the middle of your "bad" marriage?

What if the point isn't that God can tell the difference between a good and bad marriage, but that He's more interested in handcrafting "bad" marriages where He gets seen as good, loving, sovereign, and wise as He is? This takes place as two people who are relational polar opposites stick it out, by working through their differences and continuing to love each other, with their primary goal of glorifying Him, getting to know Him better, and as a by-product, becoming more like Him, as well as embracing the sufferings of a "bad" marriage with the hope that the rest of this broken world, who can't do marriage on their own without Him, sees it?

The question is, do you know Jesus well enough, are you experiencing His love, forgiveness, and grace to the extent that you are more motivated for His reputation than your satisfaction, comfort, and fulfillment? Which is a bigger deal, that you get satisfied or God gets glorified?

Is the well-worn maxim "happy wife, happy life" evidence of codependence, cowardice, and an unthinking consent to the curse? "You will want to control your husband."

Genesis 3:16 New English Translation

Which Is More Important to You?

Which is more important to you, "fellowshipping with his suffering" or fellowshipping with her? Philippians 3:10 says, ". . . that I may know Him and the power of His resurrection and the fellowship of His sufferings, being conformed to His death."

I am not sure if I've ever met anyone who likes the second part of this verse as much as the first. During the first years of my salvation, I heard the phrase "knowing Him and making Him known." That phrase motivated me, but somehow, successfully excluded the suffering part. I wonder if we unknowingly have done the same thing throughout our Christian life. We are massively into the feel-good first half, but somehow forget or ignore the second. And sadly, we either get confused or angry at God when He designs and implements the second half into our lives.

For the most part, when God placed the second part in my life, I ran. When things got hard, uncomfortable, uninteresting, lacked success and/or fulfillment I ran from 3:10b to something else, usually one of my many idols. God is unbelievably patient. He allows us to run from His handcrafted suffering, for a while. But then lovingly provides big fishes, forty years in the desert, Damascus Roads, or the "Hounds of Heaven" to get us back on track with His "fellowshipping."

Is there a possibility that you, like me, have attempted to use your "bad" wife as an escape from 3:10b? You wanted to know Jesus and His resurrection power, but when He stuck in the suffering part, you ran to her to get away from Him? Now your "escape plan" is blowing up in your face. She's not "working" anymore, and you're blaming her for not being able to get you away from His handcrafted plan of suffering for you. And because of her inability in this area, you now consider her a "bad" wife.

If we belong to Him, God doesn't give the option of part *a* with no 3:10b (Heb 12:6). Is there a possibility that God's primary way of making 3:10a into a reality is by lovingly including 3:10b? Can I say that again? Is there a possibility that God's primary way of making the first part a reality is by lovingly including the second?

So, which is more important to you, going through His handcrafted sufferings of your "bad" marriage in order to more intimately know Him, or continuing in your attempts to by-pass the fellowshipping of His suffering through fellowshipping with her?

Forgiveness has to be re-given over and over and over again (70×7).

Matthew 18:21–22

De-idolizing her will take place in the same way, most likely for years.

Matthew 19:29

Sacrifice It

"So here's what I want you to do, God helping you: Take your everyday, ordinary life—your sleeping, eating, going-to-work, and walking-around life—and place it before God as an offering. Embracing what God does for you is the best thing you can do for Him" (Rom 12:1 *The Message*).

"If you try to hang on to your life, you will lose it. But if you give up your life for My sake, you will save it" (Matt 16:25).

"Do not be anxious or worried about anything, but in everything [every circumstance and situation] by prayer and petition with thanksgiving, continue to make your [specific] requests known to God. And the peace of God [that peace which reassures the heart, that peace] which transcends all understanding, [that peace which] stands guard over your hearts and your minds in Christ Jesus [is yours]" (Phil 4:6-7 Amplified Bible).

These are fantastic verses. I want to see if I can make them practical in the context of our "bad" marriages. For a number of months now, I have been practicing what I'm now going to pass on to you. The cool thing is, it works. Here it is. Place whatever's bugging you on His alter. Whatever it is. When you find yourself being emotionally overwhelmed, panicking, fear-filled, struggling with trusting your feelings more than Him and what He said, thinking about running or cheating, cheating that possibly takes the form of an affair, divorce, chemicals, substances, pornography, or the most painful of all, wanting to run away from Jesus—whatever it is, place it on His alter. You don't have to feel it. Your emotions don't have to agree with what you're gonna say and mentally do. You are, as a matter of surrendered obedience, going to sacrifice it. Please reread the verses I placed at the beginning of this section.

I did that on purpose. I wanted God's word to be the foundation for what's gonna happen here. This works. It's simple, but it works.

Let me give you an example. The other day it seemed like God was showing me from my early morning time with Him and throughout the day that I can't do anything on my own (Matt 5:3; John 15:5). The words from these verses are pretty casual to read, but terribly painful to live. I'm not going to bore you with the details, but absolutely everything I tried that day blew up. Nothing worked. I became overwhelmed and unbelievably discouraged. It was at that point that it seemed like God brought up in my time alone with Him Matthew 5:3: "Blessed are those who realize their need for Him." Even though my emotions were nowhere close to agreeing with what I was going to do, I said, "To the best of my ability, with everything I have in me right now, Abba, I sacrifice, I lay on Your altar, any and all of the abilities You've given me. Apart from You, I can't do anything. I want You more than I want success and accomplishment. Thank You for accepting my sacrifice." It took a while, and I can't even give an exact time, but the anxiety and funk left.

Now I don't know how weird this sounds to you, but it's really weird to me. That Matthew 16 verse is not easy. I mean, how do you let go of your past, your goals, your long-held fantasies and desires? How do I let go of my yesterday passions for God's today will? Here it is, sacrifice it! With the belief that as I let go of my old stuff, He'll replace it with His John 10:10 "abundant life" new stuff. You don't have to feel it. Your emotions don't have to agree with what your mind, will, and words are saying. Just sacrifice it! Whatever that thing is that's stealing your peace and joy, sacrifice it! Give it to Him! You may not, and most likely won't, feel it while you're doing it, but that's not important. Sacrifice it! And as you lay it on His alter, "the peace of God which surpasses all understanding will take over your heart and mind." Sacrifice it!

What would happen if when we read the Bible,
we believed what it said?
"Every good and perfect gift is from above."

James 1:17

"A wise, understanding, and sensible wife is [a gift and blessing] from the Lord." The Message Translation

Proverbs 19:14

Suffering

It's fairly easy to write, but impossible to do any of the stuff I've been suggesting in this little book unless Jesus does it in and through us. The directive in Ephesians 5 that says we husbands are to "love your wives, just as Christ loved the church and gave Himself up for her" is one of those directives. How could anyone love anyone the way Christ loved them (Eph 5:25–30)? How could we as husbands give ourselves to our wives in the exact same way, to the exact same extent that Jesus gave Himself for the church? Without grace and the Holy Spirit doing this in and through us, it's never going to happen. If you're reading this little book, and you perceive yourself as having a "bad" wife, in a "bad" marriage, there's every possibility you might be expecting, or worse demanding, that she "give herself up" for you rather than the other way around? Is there a possibility, that you're experiencing suffering in your marriage because you're not loving your "bad" wife the way Jesus loves her?

I'm unbelievably grateful for the insight and instruction from God's word in Ephesians 5:25–30. But again, I find it impossible to live these Ephesian 5 directives out on a consistent basis. If I make it three days in a row of even getting close to partially living this out toward my wife, I'm grateful to God and my wife is grateful to Him as well. To love my wife the way Jesus loves His church is impossible to do . . . without God doing it through me. Too much pain. Too much suffering. Too much inadequacy. Too much selfishness. Too much, me-first-ness.

I think the only thing I can do at this point, in the writing of this little section, is to pray and ask forgiveness for my sin of self-centeredness and my demanding my plan over His for my marriage. And at the same time thank God for His grace that makes it possible and gives me hope that He can and will live out through me, this Ephesians 5 "great mystery," for and toward my "bad" wife.

Prayer: Jesus, I'm a complete mess. I am so selfish and so self-centered. I haven't sacrificed for my wife. I've demanded that she sacrifice for me. I've demanded that she love me like You love Your church. God I'm so grateful that You love me just as much as You love Jesus (John 17). And I'd ask that You miraculously take the love You've given me and pass it on to my wife through me. I'd ask that in Your power, someday You will give me the ability to daily love her the way You've already loved and have always loved her, me, and Your church. Thank You for listening, Jesus.

You are my source. She is my *You*-given resource of joy and companionship.

Psalm 16:11

Suffering II

Some forty years ago in my New Testament Survey class, on the first day of class during the introduction, Dr. Eckman, my professor, said something like, "Some of you may be wondering what God's will for your life is. Well, you're standing in it." Basically, what he was saying was that God doesn't have plan Bs. If "you're standing in it," that's God's plan A for your life. Proverbs 16:33 says that He controls everything, even something as inconsequential as the outcome of rolling dice.

Since this is true, how can you and I consider the possibility that our marriages aren't God's will? When we think this, what we're actually saying is that our "bad" marriage is the first mistake God ever made. What we're saying is that our plan A is better than God's plan A.

Sovereignty. That's a big church word that means God's in charge of everything. Basically, everything He wants to happen happens and nothing He doesn't want to happen ever happens. Revelation 13:10 says, "Anyone who is destined for prison will be taken to prison. Anyone destined to die by the sword will die by the sword." Many other verses throughout the Bible state that whatever God has determined for us, whatever His plan A is, is going to happen. In the context of this little book, you may not like it, and it may not be your plan A, but if you are wondering what God's will is for your "bad" marriage, "you're standing in it."

"The Lord will work out His plans for my 'bad' marriage" (paraphrased from Ps 138:8).

Nothing can separate me from His love.
Not even my "bad" marriage.

Romans 8:31–39

Pain

I've often said that pain and suffering are my best friends. I'm taking this from the two companions of Much Afraid; Suffering and Sorrow, from the insight-filled book *Hinds' Feet on High Places*, by Hannah Hurnard.

Pain is God's alarm clock to wake up a "bad" marriage." In the context of marriage and almost every other area in life, we believe that "if it ain't broke, don't fix it." Pain is the grace-filled marital microphone God uses to let us know our marriage is broke and needs fixing. The problem with most of us is, we view the person God is using to wake us up as an enemy rather than a God-ordained tool in His plan to make us more like Him through our "bad" marriage. We end up blaming her and Him for His handcrafted pain and then look for ways to run from rather than humbly go through that pain.

Too many times we view our marriages as an FIY project with a "some assembly required" notice rather than a "do not try this at home" and "read the owner's manual" warning (Ps 40:1–5). We get ourselves in pain-filled situations because we're hanging on to our plan for our marriage and then create even more pain when we try to do it ourselves in our power. When it blows up, we blame God and our "bad" wives for our idolatrous plans, attempted in our anemic power. Proverbs 19:3 says, "People ruin their lives by their own foolishness and then are angry at the Lord." That's exactly what's happening when we run from and attempt to blame our "bad" wives for God's loudspeaker.

What I'm hoping for in this little book is that the pain you're currently experiencing in your "bad" marriage will motivate you to cry out to Jesus, your number one love, and ask Him to get your

JUST LOVE HER

relationship with Him back on track (2 Cor 11:3). Next, pray that God would restore your second most important relationship with her (Mal 2:13-16; 1 Pet 3:7). Then consider reading the Bible with a priority of learning and experiencing God's amazing, no-strings-attached, perfect, unconditional love for you. Experiencing this love will give comfort during your times of pain, knowing that He has a purpose for the pain and that you are not alone in it.

Most everything I talk about in this book is going to be marinated in pain. Lots and lots of it. Thank goodness that God doesn't waste pain. He always recycles it into something that's good for us and glorifies Him. Always!

Could loving your "bad" wife be a daily "living sacrifice, holy and well-pleasing to God, which is your rational [logical, intelligent] act of worship"?

Romans 12:1 Amplified Bible

Pain II

I wonder how many of us came to Jesus (i.e., Jesus began living inside of us) with the internal, unspoken reservation of, "as long as You make my life better, as long as You supercharge my success, as long as You make my life more comfortable, as long as I set my goals and You help me accomplish them, I'll give my life to You?"

Now I know that sounds ugly, but I'm pretty sure that's the way I came to Jesus. I was dating the love of my life at the time, Donna, while a junior in high school. Donna said there was a chance that I got her pregnant. After hearing this news, I was more afraid of my father cutting off body parts than I was of going to hell. But, for the first time in my life, I was convinced I was a sinner. At that point I said, "Jesus, if You're for real, would You come into my life and take away my sins?" Those are the exact, out-loud words I used back in 1977. But what I "said" in an internal, unknown-at-the-time, mental-whisper was, "As long as You give me someone as good as or better than Donna, I'll give my life to You, Jesus."

What I didn't know then, but know now, showed where my heart was at and what my first passion was: female companionship. What I was actually saying was, "Yes God, I'll give You my life, as long as . . ." This little pre-salvific, dual-love, contractual condition I placed on God back then is the same one I placed on my "bad" wife without knowing it almost twenty-five years ago.

Much of the pain in our "bad" marriages with our "bad" wives is a by-product of our dual loves. In the same way the Bible says we can't love God and money (Luke 6:13), you can't have a dual-love relationship with God and anything or anyone else. My dual love of God and women, of God and marriage, of God and sex, of God and romance, has caused pain and problems in my relationships with God and my "bad" wife.

The Bible calls my sinful priority of women idolatry. Again, an idol is any person, place, position, possession, or thing that either shares or takes my first-place space from Jesus. An idol is that thing that I run to instead of Jesus to meet my primary, God-given needs. The problem with idolatry is, idols work until they don't. The reason they eventually don't work is because they can't handle the pressure of being in that number-one-need-meeter slot. Jesus is the only one that can stand in our God-shaped, God-created, need-meeter slot.

My woman-idolatry worked, until I got married. After marriage, the "unspoken" condition, demand, passion I placed on Jesus so long ago was now the unconscious condition I placed on and now demanded of my new wife. The same thing I said to Jesus was now the unspoken, and at that time, unknown condition I placed on my wife, Laurie. The condition said, "As long as you meet my previously unmet needs as good as or better than my last idol, you're good. If not, you're 'bad.' And if 'bad,' I'm going to spend the rest of our marriage reminding you of your 'badness' with my nitpicking, faultfinding, and resentment-keeping because you didn't meet the unspoken, unrealistic expectations I placed on you."

This is one of the places the pain you're currently experiencing in your marriage comes from. We have attempted to get this God-can-only-meet need met, from something other than God. And in the context of this little book, that other-than-God thing we're placing our unrealistic expectations on is our "bad" wife. Whenever we want something more and/or different than what Jesus wants for us, there's always going to be pain. He loves us too much to allow us to be distracted by some smaller-than-Him thing (Ps 16; 2 Cor 11:3).

JUST LOVE HER

Expose yourself. Bring it into the light. Ask out loud for help for your "bad" marriage before it's too late. "Is anyone among you suffering? He must pray. Is anyone joyful? He is to sing praises [to God]. Is anyone among you sick? He must call for the elders (spiritual leaders) of the church and they are to pray over him, anointing him with oil in the name of the Lord; and the prayer of faith will restore the one who is sick, and the Lord will raise him up; and if he has committed sins, he will be forgiven. Therefore, confess your sins to one another [your false steps, your offenses], and pray for one another, that you may be healed and restored. The heartfelt and persistent prayer of a righteous man (believer) can accomplish much [when put into action and made effective by God—it is dynamic and can have tremendous power]" (Jas 5:13-16 Amplified Bible).

Pain III

There is an anonymous quote which says, "Pain is inevitable, but suffering is optional." Life is difficult and pain is just an everyday part of it. Suffering on the other hand is a by-product of my perception of that pain. Other than the spiritual metamorphosis that takes place at our salvation (2 Cor 5:17) pain is the number one tool God uses to make us look like Him (Rom 5:3-5; Jas 1:2-4). In the context of our "bad" marriages, I wonder if it's possible to have a biblical perception of God's design for pain in our "bad" marriages.

Some God-designed pain passages say things like, our current sufferings are not equal to our future time with Jesus; we not only get to believe in Jesus but we get to suffer as well; we not only get to know Jesus, we get to share His sufferings; we speak highly of our suffering because it develops character; because Jesus left an example of suffering for us, we will suffer as well; God is pleased with us when we patiently endure undeserved suffering; and finally it is necessary to go through various trials (1 Pet 1:6; 2 Tim 3:12; Acts 9:16; Rom 8:18; Phil 1:29; Phil 3:10; Rom 5:3; 1 Pet 2:20-21).

I could keep going, since the word *suffering*, in various forms, is used nearly two hundred times in the Bible. A possible problem you and I might have with these references is we have spiritually selective hearing. If you're like me, you love highlighting the verses of Jesus' unconditional love and acceptance, along with verses that talk about God kicking our enemy's rear ends and those verses that talk about His power that's available to us. But when it comes to highlighting verses that show our need to go through pain and suffering, we tend to pass on the highlighting. Pain and suffering don't fit in with our unspoken "God's here to make my life easier, more comfortable and more successful" mindset. Suffering verses don't fit the bargaining strategy we had with Jesus when we first met.

But if it's true, that pain is God's loudspeaker to wake me up to the reality that something's wrong with my "bad" marriage, it might also be true that pain is God's tool for change. To the degree that our heart, our mindset, our agenda, our passions lineup with His, the pain will be more about getting to know and please Him, and less about suffering. As we, with God's help, develop not just the mindset, but a heartset that says, "What You will. When You will. How You will," the pain we experience will now have a purpose and be a bit easier to endure.

This poem by an unknown author seems to attempt to present a "fellowship of His sufferings," and a "3:10b" motivation to persist through our God-designed pain. This poem may even provide insight on what He might be doing through our "bad" marriages. It says,

> When God wants to drill a man and thrill a man and skill a man,
> When God wants to mold a man to play the noblest part;
> When He yearns with all His heart to create so great and bold a man
> That all the world shall praise ... watch His methods; watch His ways!
> How He ruthlessly perfects whom He royally elects ...
> How He hammers him and hurts him
> and the mighty blows converts him
> Into frail shapes of clay that only God understands.
> How his tortured heart is crying and he lifts beseeching hands...
> How He bends but never breaks, when his good He undertakes,
> How He uses whom He chooses...with every purpose fuses him;
> By every art induces him to try His splendor out ...
> God knows what He's about.

Is there a possibility that what you're calling love, is actually "obsession" and idolatry?

2 Samuel 13

Pain IV

Sacrifice is not one of my favorite words or behaviors. But when you combine "living" and "sacrifice" from Romans 12:1, to this pain-principle thing, it begins to sound chronically nasty.

Have you ever wished that this 12:1 verse wouldn't apply to you? If you belong to Jesus and if He lives inside of you, the whole Bible applies to you, including this verse and others like it. Sadly, we don't get to salad-bar the Bible. It doesn't matter whether I choose to hear the suffering passages or not, God and His handcrafted plan for my "bad" marriage is going to get applied to me, whether I like it or not. Pain helps me see that it's broken. And if I don't see that my "bad" marriage is broken, I ain't gonna try to fix it.

Does "all those who are Godly in Christ Jesus will suffer" (2 Tim 3:12) apply to you? Does 12:1, "living and holy sacrifice," apply to you? Why wouldn't they apply to the hardest "spiritual service of worship" God ever created, my "bad" marriage? Of course, they do.

Don't be scared. Like everything else in this book, this "living sacrifice" thing is impossible without Jesus doing it in and through us. God has never directed us to do anything without the underlying promise that He will do it for and through us (Ps 127:1).

I choose to suffer for my "bad" wife in our "bad" marriage because I am a Christian-marriage-martyr. Jesus did it for His church, He will empower me to do it for my "bad" wife.

Ephesians 5:25

I Choose to Suffer Because . . .

I choose to suffer in my "bad" marriage. What's my alternative? Divorce? Affairs? Extramarital exploits? Pornography? Chemicals? Daily drunks? Other dumb stuff? Nope. I choose to suffer in my "bad" marriage because:

1. "He (Jesus) learned trusting-obedience by what He suffered, just as we do" (Heb 5:8 *The Message*). Why wouldn't this apply to my "bad" marriage?"
2. "Everyone who wants to live a godly life in Christ Jesus will suffer" (2 Tim 3:12). Why wouldn't this apply to my "bad" marriage?"
3. "It is better to suffer for doing good, if that is what God wants" (1 Pet 3:17). Why wouldn't this apply to my "bad" marriage?"
4. "Our present troubles are small and won't last very long. Yet they produce for us a glory that vastly outweighs them and will last forever?" (2 Cor 4:17; Matt 22:30). Why wouldn't this apply to my "bad" marriage?"
5. Being "patient and kind" isn't easy for me (1 Cor 13:4). Why wouldn't this apply to my "bad" marriage?"
6. I'm prone to being "jealous" (1 Cor 13:4). Why wouldn't this apply to my "bad" marriage?"
7. I tend to be "arrogant," "boastful," "proud," and "rude." It's hard to keep my mouth shut and my heart selfless (1 Cor 13:5; Phil 2:3). Why wouldn't this apply to my "bad" marriage?"
8. I tend to be snarky and a nitpicker (1 Cor 13:5). Why wouldn't this apply to my "bad" marriage?"

9. I tend to be a quitter and lack fortitude (1 Cor 13:7; Rom 5:3–5; Jas 1:3–4). Why wouldn't this apply to my "bad" marriage?"

10. You will help me through each and every one of my troubles (Ps 34:19 Living Bible). Why wouldn't this apply to my "bad" marriage?"

11. "As far as we are concerned we do not wish to stand in anyone's way, nor do we wish to bring discredit on the ministry God has given us. Indeed we want to prove ourselves genuine ministers of God whatever we have to go through—patient endurance of troubles or even disasters, being flogged or imprisoned; being mobbed, having to work like slaves, having to go without food or sleep. All this we want to meet with sincerity, with insight and patience; by sheer kindness and the Holy Spirit; with genuine love, speaking the plain truth, and living by the power of God. Our sole defense, our only weapon, is a life of integrity, whether we meet honor or dishonor, praise or blame. Called "impostors" we must be true, called "nobodies" we must be in the public eye. Never far from death, yet here we are alive, always "going through it" yet never "going under". We know sorrow, yet our joy is inextinguishable. We have "nothing to bless ourselves with" yet we bless many others with true riches. We are penniless, and yet in reality we have everything worth having" (2 Cor 6:3–10, J. B. Phillips Translation). Why wouldn't this apply to my "bad" marriage?"

12. You (Jesus) suffered at the hands of the one you loved, served, and washed his feet (John 13:4–5). Why wouldn't this apply to my "bad" marriage?"

13. My "bad" wife, my neighbors, my town, my state, my country, and eventually my world and even the angels will see and experience how much Jesus loves them through my sufferings for them (Col 1:24; 1 Pet 1:12; Acts 1:8; Rom 5:10). Why wouldn't this apply to my "bad" marriage?"

JUST LOVE HER

God using and blessing the sufferings of those who suffer is not limited to pastors, missionaries, and the super-spiritual with super-cool callings. They apply to anyone who is attempting to obey their God-given calling in whatever field, position, profession, relationship God has called them to. Why wouldn't this apply to my "bad" marriage?"

Yep! I choose to suffer because He "who makes everything holy and whole, [makes] you holy and whole, put[s] you together—spirit, soul, and body—and keep[s] you fit for the coming of our Master, Jesus Christ. The One who called you is completely dependable. If He said it, He'll do it! (1 Thess 5:23–24 *The Message*). Why wouldn't this apply to my "bad" marriage?"

Please consider reading chapter 10 on suffering from *Desiring God*, by John Piper. Seriously! You won't be disappointed, and God might use this book and this chapter to help you choose to suffer for your "bad" wife and your "bad" marriage.

You forgave me. I forgive her.

Proverbs 17:9

Forgiveness

It is impossible to *just love her* without forgiving her. I once heard someone say something like, "Anytime humans are involved, there's going to be a mess." One of the problems with messes is they hurt. If the hurts from the relational messes aren't dealt with healthfully, they fester, get ugly, and turn into resentments. Resentments are relational viruses that if left alone always pass from the people we "hate" to the ones we love. Relational messes are the equivalent of relational dung piles. Most people walk around piles like these. But, when we're stuck in resentment, we can't help ourselves, we repeatedly walk right through them. Many times, we purposely create these piles so we can purposely walk through. An example of this is every time we bring up her past while in an argument. Another way we continue to walk through the piles is to nitpick and allow annoyances to become mountains instead of remaining relational molehills. The primary way to walk around these piles is forgiveness.

    I want to apply the thought that "you can't give what you don't have, not even to yourself," to this section on forgiveness. To the degree you've experience and accepted God's "it is finished" forgiveness, to that same degree you now have His amazing grace-filled forgiveness to give to her and others. To the degree you have relinquished all performance-oriented, do-more-try-harder penance and chosen to rest in and rely on His finished work on the cross (Heb 10:10, 12), forgiveness, to that same degree you will be able to pass it on to her.

    A simple illustration of this would be if I were to say, "Give me a glass of water." Very simply, if you don't have a glass of water, you can't give it to me. It's the same thing with forgiveness. If you haven't received it, you can't give it. To the degree, based on the quality of the forgiveness you've received, to that same degree you will then and only then have that quality of forgiveness to extend to your "bad" wife.

This "you can't give what you don't have" thing might be difficult for you to take in. The reality is that everyone knows they need to forgive. That's relational kindergartner stuff. The simple question is, why don't you? You know you're supposed to, but why haven't you forgiven? Is there a possibility you don't have what it takes?

For the most part, many if not most Christians, other than what they experienced at salvation, are not experiencing God's true forgiveness. That doesn't mean God's forgiveness isn't currently active and available, it just means many if not most Christians aren't experiencing it. Many Christians stumble over the same "stone" the Jews stumbled over (Rom 9:30–33). They attempt to earn as a "spiritual paycheck" that forgiveness that can only be received as a free gift (Col 2:21–23; Titus 3:5). They have adopted an unbiblical belief that God's forgiveness is based on the "rights" they do and "wrongs" they don't (Gal 1:1–9; 3:1–4).

For many Christians the earning and performing takes the form of doing religious activities such as going to church, putting money in a plate, getting up early and reading the Bible, praying on their knees, journaling, or helping folks across the street, etc. You might be thinking, "What's wrong with that? Those are all good things." Nothing's wrong with these activities. Unless you're attempting to earn through performance the forgiveness God's already given for free (Rom 3:20, 22; Gal 5:1; Eph 2:8–9). Here's the hiccup, all these efforts at earning and performing have a cost.

Relationally speaking, the cost of your not receiving as a gift, but attempting to earn through performance, the forgiveness God has already provided for free, will end up being the same standard you place on your "bad" wife. You will demand, either spoken or not, that she does all the right stuff and none of the wrong, in order for her to earn, not receive as an undeserved gift, the "forgiveness" you're lending her, with interest. This performance-for-forgiveness standard is a by-product of your not receiving (you can't give what you don't have) as a gift, God's forgiveness. And sadly, you're now in the process of destroying your marriage because you can't, don't, or won't forgive, because you don't have what it takes.

Romans 3:23–24 says, "For everyone has sinned; we all fall short of God's glorious standard. Yet God, in His grace, freely makes us right in His sight. He did this through Christ Jesus when He freed us from the penalty for our sins." These verses are amazing. There's no penance, no earning, no performing, just "grace" that's "freely given," that "makes us right in His sight." Obviously there are tons of other verses in the Bible that talk about God freely forgiving us; but I love these because they're so simple, straightforward and make it clear there's no earning or performing involved with receiving and experiencing God's forgiveness.

There's something else about v. 23. It says that "everyone has sinned; we all fall short." This verse is an objective reminder that everyone's a mess and causes messes. Everyone is a sinner. If you are not forgiving your "bad" wife and holding onto resentments, you have forgotten who God says you are—a forgiven sinner. It doesn't matter what she's done, you are just as big a sinner as she is. You both are in need of God's grace and forgiveness. Remembering this sin principle might make it easier to forgive her and let the resentments go.

Here's another thought from Ephesians 5:25–26. It says that you're supposed to be willing to give your life for her. It's nearly impossible to be willing to die for someone you're holding a grudge against. So, again, which is more important to you, what she did, or what He says? Let it go. In His power, forgive her.

Here's a few other verses that give snippets of what we experience, and now "have" to give when we are forgiven. Remembering, "you can't give what you don't have."

Hebrews 9:12; 10:10, 12 states that the forgiveness God has given us and we already have, covers all our sins, past, present, and future, "forever."

Micah 7:19 states that because of the forgiveness God has given us, and we already have, He throws all our sins into the deepest sea.

Hebrews 8:12 states that because of the forgiveness that God has given us, and we already have, He chooses to forget, and He never again remembers our sin. The sins I chose not to forget (resentments) are the sins He has already chosen to forgive and forget.

Isaiah 1:18 states that the forgiveness God has given us, and we already have, makes our past, nasty, ugly, shame-filled sin pure, "as white as wool."

Romans 5:1 states that the forgiveness God has given us, and we already have, makes us best friends (righteous) with Jesus through what He did for us, not for what we do for Him.

Romans 5:20 states that the forgiveness through grace that God has given us, and we already have, is supersized—bigger than any sins we have committed.

So, since we already have God's "it is finished" forgiveness through His grace, we now have resentment-killing forgiveness to pass on to our "bad" wives.

It's not about her transformation but both of our resting in and relying on His substitutionary work for the both of us.

> "Accept His worthiness for my unworthiness, His sinlessness for my transgressions, His purity for my uncleanness, His sincerity for my guile, His truth for my deceits, His meekness for my pride, His constancy for my backslidings, His love for my enmity, His fullness for my emptiness, His faithfulness for my treachery, His obedience for my lawlessness, His glory for my shame, His devotedness for my waywardness, His holy life for my unchaste ways, His righteousness for my dead works, His death for my life."
>
> *Puritan prayer (author unknown)*

Forgiveness II

There's a lot of confusion out there regarding forgiveness. One of the worst misconceptions is the belief that says, "I can forgive myself." If this is something you believe as a Christian, I'm sorry. Somehow you got seriously off track. I would encourage you to try and find anywhere in the Bible that says you can forgive yourself. This, I believe, is a humanistic belief that is completely unbiblical. There's only One who can forgive sins and that's Jesus (Luke 5:21). You can remind yourself that Jesus forgave you, but there is no true forgiveness apart from Him or in this belief.

Next, anytime I do something wrong, somebody has to pay for it. This kinda goes along with the previous belief of being able to forgive yourself. An example of this is when I was going to school in Denver, I drove to work every day with a coworker in his little Datsun pickup. His daily routine was to stop at a local convenience store, walk in and grab three Hostess treats and a very large Slurpee, without paying for any of it. After about the third day of this routine, I said, "Dude, you didn't pay for any of that." His response was, "Ah, it's no big deal. They have insurance." This response apparently worked for him. But in reality, he wasn't paying for his breakfast, 7-Eleven was.

When I sin and don't admit it, confess it (to them and God), and attempt to fix or make amends, I'm making whoever I hurt pay for my misdeed/sin. I'm telling the one(s) I hurt, "Deal with it." "I already forgave myself." "I hope you have insurance." Ouch!

So, what's the big deal? Since we can only pass on to others the forgiveness we have accepted and experienced from God, I can tell myself all day long that "I forgave myself," but in reality, I still don't have the authority to forgive myself or the wherewithal to forgive my "bad" wife because I've never truly either been forgiven (non-Christian) or am resting in and experiencing His true forgiveness I've already been given (Rom 3:24; 5:1).

This is one of the reasons so many people know they should forgive, but still can't, because they still have nothing to give. The ones I hurt and sinned against are still paying and I'm building up a guilty conscience. And the ones who have hurt me are still paying because I have no (usable) forgiveness to pass on to them. I can tell myself and others that "I forgave myself," but God, Jesus, the Holy Spirit, and the scriptures are pretty hard to lie to.

For years in counseling sessions, I have attempted to try and help confused Christians who have attempted to live out this belief. There is an authentic biblical alternative. Based on what the Bible says and what Jesus has already done on the cross, every time I sin I can agree with God that what I did was sin (1 John 1:9). I then can remind myself that Jesus has already forgiven me whenever a sense of false guilt or a drive to earn my forgiveness pops up. He has already provided His once-for-all-time, "it is finished" sacrifice for all my sins, past, present, and future (Heb 9:12; 10: 10, 12). I can also attempt to make amends, confess and ask forgiveness from the person I hurt (Jas 5:16; Matt 5:23-24). God is the One that forgives me but attempting to make amends is a helpful way of not making the ones I hurt "pay" for what I did to them. A clear conscience is priceless and powerful, especially in the context of *just loving her* and others.

Another forgiveness confusion suggests that "if I forgive what they did, it means I condone it." There's this wonderfully grace-filled example in John 8:1-11. In it, there was a woman caught in adultery. The Jewish law said she needed to be killed for this sin. Jesus extended forgiveness to her, but in v. 11 He said, "Go and sin no more." Jesus didn't condone what she did, but He did forgive her. Using Jesus' example, and in His power, I'll want to do the same thing with my "bad" wife (Eph 4:32).

Another simple illustration of this would be my going 30 in a 20-mph school zone with my wife in the car. I sinned by breaking the law and getting a $120 fine for my negligence. My wife isn't pleased and is certainly not condoning what I did. And I'm pretty sure she hopes I never do it again. But she very graciously forgives me and says, "It's no big deal." She then also promptly reminds me that we'll be eating Ramon Noodles for the next three months. This never happened, but it's a simple example of forgiving without condoning.

The next hiccup in the context of forgiveness is, "I have to feel forgiving before I can give forgiveness." Nope. Forgiveness is just like love; I don't have to feel it in order to extend it. Forgiveness is a choice. It's a decision. I choose to forgive based on the fact that God tells me to forgive others and has already forgiven me (Eph 4:32; Phil 4:32). Since God has already forgiven me for all the horrible sins I've done, I can now pass that same forgiveness on to my "bad" wife for the minuscule things she has done, whether I feel forgiving or not (Rom 15:7).

Again, we place too much faith in our feelings. We get a sense that we're either being fake or hypocritical if we don't feel something before we do it. Feelings have nothing to do with forgiveness (Col 3:13). There may be a sense of joy, relief, and contentment after forgiving her, but there's no emotional prerequisite before forgiving her (Gen 4:7).

The next hiccup in the context of forgiveness is "if I don't forget it, I didn't give it." Bummer. This notion can be really disturbing, draining, and disruptive in our "bad" marriages. Why? Because marriage really hurts. Even when you love someone, you're still going to hurt them and they're going to hurt you. Remember that whenever there are humans involved there's going to be messes. And some of those messes really hurt and are going to be really hard to forget.

I wish I could forget a lot of my past junk. But forgiving is far more important than forgetting. And in reality, there's a far better chance I'll forget it, if I forgive it. The priority is to forgive (1 Pet 4:8). I wonder if this is why Jesus said to forgive seventy times seven if necessary (Matt 18:21-22). Why? Because many times, the ones who hurt us keep hurting us and keep making that same mess that's really hard to forget. The hope or goal here is that every time a painful memory of that experience comes to mind, I can tell myself, "God's already forgiven me for all my junk, and I've already forgiven her for hers." And if necessary, I continue to do this seventy times seven, or for however long my inability to forget lasts; possibly for the rest of my life.

We may struggle with the inability to forget our and her past sins. God on the other hand does not. Hebrews 8:12 says, "I will remember their sins no more." Let's look at this for a second. Recall the worst sin you ever committed. You got yours, I got mine. At times that nasty thing jumps into my memory without any effort at all on my part. I'm really grateful that God forgave me for that. But even more than that, He chooses not to remember it. He throws my sin into the deepest sea and chooses not to remember it (Mic 7:9; Heb 8:12).

Now, as we said before, the only forgiveness we can pass on to others is the forgiveness we experience. You can't give what you don't have, not even to yourself, let alone your "bad" wife. Since the forgiveness you have been given from God is the forgiveness where He chooses not to remember your sin, in the same way, you can now ask Him to help you choose to forget your "bad" wife's sin. The sins I can't forget are the sins He has chosen not to remember. Thank God this applies to the both of us! Now, in His power pass it on to her.

And finally in the context of forgiveness, many times we "lend" forgiveness rather than give it. What I mean by this is every time you bring up a "forgiven" past, what you're actually saying is, "Even though I told you I forgave you, I actually just let you borrow that 'forgiveness' until I might need to bring it up again in order to either win a future argument or feel a sense of unhealthy control." True, authentic forgiveness needs to be given over and over again, never lent. It's that seventy times seven thing again.

The past memories, emotions, and pain of previous forgivings will come up again and again, especially in the middle of a disagreement. The goal here is to keep reminding ourselves that God forgave us of our grossest sins, so we'll want to do the same for our "bad" wife (Prov 17:9). Putting authentic forgiveness into practice, with God's help, in His power, is a wonderful way to *just love her*.

Jesus, I don't understand what You are doing in my "bad" marriage. Many times I would rather die than live in this pain. But I trust You and Your plan and choose to believe that You are good, wise, and all-powerful in the middle of my pain.

Luke 22:42

Resentments

Selfishness is the #1 cause of relational breakups. Selfishness is the me-first mindset that says, "You're here for me." This is a resentment waiting to happen. Why? Because eventually it's not going to happen. People don't get married to have a one-way, all-taking-and-no-giving relationship. This "it's all about me," "you're here for me," self-centered mindset is an example of an unhealthy, unrealistic expectation.

Most of the time these unrealistic expectations (UEs), are unspoken, and look something like, "I got married so that you would meet my needs." Or "you are here to make me successful, to make my plans work and fulfill my relational fantasies."

I once heard someone say that "expectations are the mother of resentments." I'm not sure who said it, but I agree with them. When you find yourself feeling resentment, given enough time and effort, you can usually trace it back to UEs. The explanation is fairly simple. I expect you, my "bad" wife, to do x, y, and z for me. If you can't, don't, or won't, I'll hold it against you. I'll say something like, "All I'm seeing is relational false advertising. You looked and sounded like you could do _____ for me, but now I think we both know that's not gonna happen." Or "I'm supposed to give up my dreams, my goals, and my fantasies for you. I don't think so." My unfulfilled UEs have now birthed resentments toward my "bad" wife. That's one of the reasons selfishness is so dangerous and resentments are so common.

Another thought with this resentment thing is that not even God was willing to fulfill our x, y, and z. You tried. You prayed. You asked God for these things and He either said no, or was moving too slowly, or was in the process of actually removing, not providing

Just Love Her

them. Since God didn't do it, now it's her turn. You're expecting, unrealistically, that she do for you what God was unwilling to do. You are demanding that she be your relational savior. Jesus is our only Savior, relationally or otherwise. To ask her to do what God was unwilling to do is a major UE and eventual resentment.

Again, going back to the thought that resentments are relational viruses, that if not dealt with healthfully, through authentic grace and forgiveness, spread from the person we "hate," to the one(s) we love. Resentment is an unhealthy form of relational control. I get to view myself as better than you because of what you did to me. Now you're just a _____ because of what you did to me. I now get to caricature or one-dimensionalize and label you as a liar, a cheat, a gossip, a whatever. And now, because you are who you are and I'm the one you did it too, I can justify my resentment-filled, unhealthy attempts to control you through my holding onto whatever it was you did to me.

Dr. Wilson in her wonderful book *Hurt People Hurt People* writes, "Resentment and bitterness are malevolent forms of interpersonal attachment-like being tied with barbed wire to people who hurt us.[6]" In other words, we use resentment to perpetuate the hurt-filled relationship, but on our terms. We get to view ourselves as better than the perpetrator due to our constant reminders of and mental playbacks (many times unconscious) of the offender's wrongful words, actions, or deeds toward us.

An example of this would be the Sunday afternoon I was watching football with my son Sammy. My wife was walking back and forth in front of the television and for whatever reason, I was mentally nitpicking on her. Obviously this wasn't out loud. But there was no reasonable reason for the nitpicking. Initially I had no clue where this was coming from. And suddenly, in the middle of the game, I asked myself, "Don, how long has it been since you talked to Dad?"

---

6. Taken from Hurt People Hurt People: Hope and Healing for Yourself and Your Relationships by Sandra D. Wilson ©200 I. Used by permission of Our Daily Bread Publishing, Box 3566, Grand Rapids, MI 49501. All rights reserved.

Just Love Her

So, what does my dad have to do with my nitpicking on Laurie? Throughout my life, my primary source of undealt-with anger and resentments has been my father. My resentments stem from the abuses my mother and all five of us kids experienced from him while growing up. So, going back to that earlier maxim, he has been the one I have "hated" and due to my neglect of maintaining a God-empowered, forgiveness-filled, relationship with him, the resentment I've had toward him was now "spreading to the one I loved," Laurie.

So, asking myself, "Don, how long has it been since you talked to your dad?"—I hadn't. Not for at least a month or longer. So, I went into a secluded room and made a call to dad. The conversation was polite, respectful, and at the end, I told him, "Love you, Dad." I then went back to watching the game, with no situational change, just an attitudinal and perspective change. Everything was "right as rain." No more nitpicking on Laurie, and actually I had a more grateful and intensified love for her.

I have You!
"I have called you by name, you are Mine."

Isaiah 43:1

Resentments II

I want to see if I can take this resentment thing a little further by looking at a couple of verses that I think address this issue. Ephesians 4:26-7 in the Amplified Version reads, "Be angry [at sin—at immorality, at injustice, at ungodly behavior], yet do not sin; do not let your anger [cause you shame, nor allow it to] last until the sun goes down. And do not give the devil an opportunity [to lead you into sin by holding a grudge, or nurturing anger, or harboring resentment, or cultivating bitterness]."

In the context of these verses, God through Paul is telling us to deal with our hurts, anger, and perceived injustices in order to keep resentment from happening. These verses are telling us to deal with the primary symptom of resentment, which in this case is anger. (You might want to go back and look at the Relational Iceberg to help see this more clearly. Anger is the *what*, resentment is the *why*.) Anyway, the goal here is to not allow the devil the opportunity to create a resentment in us toward our "bad" wife. Why? Because resentment is so powerful and destructive, it, like quick-drying cement, can solidify overnight and be really hard to deal with not only the next morning, but possibly for the rest of your life. So don't let the sun go down on your anger so that resentment doesn't set in.

Next, in Matthew 6:14-15 there are a couple confusing verses. These are verses that unhealthy controllers and spiritual abusers love to use. I'm looking at these verses in this section because I believe they deal more with potential resentment than with God somehow taking back or lending us His forgiveness.

In the NLT version it reads, "If you forgive those who sin against you, your heavenly Father will forgive you. But if you refuse to forgive others, your Father will not forgive your sins." The reason these verses are confusing is because they're confusing. They don't match up with what the rest of the Bible says about the permanence of God's forgiveness.

Back in Bible college when we were being taught how to read and study the Bible (hermeneutics), a number of our professors gave us this little quote. Now remember I'm old and it's been years since my early college days, but it went something like, "If the plain sense of Scripture doesn't make sense, seek another sense." What they were saying was, "If what you're reading matches up with the rest of Scripture, great. Stick with it. If not, do more study and figure out what God was actually saying. God never contradicts Himself and scripture always lines up with scripture. These two verses don't match up with the rest of scripture. Let me explain.

When Jesus died on the cross, His sacrifice took care of all our sins, one time, for all time. All of our sins, past, present and future, were wiped out and we were made clean, for all time. It has to be that way. Jesus only died once. He's not going to die again. It's not like in the Old Testament where every time a person sinned they had to bring a lamb and sacrifice it on the altar day after day. Unlike the little lambs in the Old Testament, Jesus only died once for all time (Heb 10:10, 12.)

The other obvious truth is, Jesus never has and never will take back the forgiveness for the sins He's already forgiven. He didn't lend us forgiveness when He died on the cross. He gave us His "it is finished," not a "stay tuned" forgiveness.

John MacArthur in his study Bible writes concerning this Matthew 6:14–15 passage,

> This is not to suggest that God will withdraw justification from those who have already received the free pardon he extends to all believers. Forgiveness in that sense—a permanent and complete acquittal from the guilt and ultimate penalty of sin—belongs to all who are in Christ. Scripture also teaches that God chastens his children who disobey. Believers are to confess their sins in order to obtain a day-to-day cleansing (1 John 1:9). This sort of forgiveness is a simple washing from the worldly

defilements of sin, not a repeat of the wholesale cleansing from sin's corruption that comes with justification. Forgiveness in this latter sense is what God threatens to withhold from Christians who refuse to forgive others.[7]

Matthew 6:14-15 in the Amplified Version reads, "For if you forgive people their trespasses [their reckless and willful sins, leaving them, letting them go, and giving up resentment], your heavenly Father will also forgive you. But if you do not forgive others their trespasses [their reckless and willful sins, leaving them, letting them go, and giving up resentment], neither will your Father forgive you your trespasses."

Let's look at this another way. The resentment-holder attempts to get the resentment-receiver to earn their forgiveness from the resentment-holder, in the same way the resentment-holder has been attempting to earn their forgiveness from the never-resentment-holding God for years. That's Matthew 6:14-15.

The problem is that much of the time the resentment-receiver can never do enough earning to get rid of the resentments being held against them by the resentment-holder. Can I say this again? The problem is that so much of the time the resentment-receiver (our "bad" wives), even if they do it perfectly (whatever it is), can never do enough earning to get rid of the resentments being held against them by the resentment-holder (us). The resentment-holder is mired in a sense of unforgiven-ness (even though it's not true) because he has never accepted and rested in God's freely given forgiveness. Because the resentment-holder isn't experiencing God's gift-form-only forgiveness, he and his "bad" wife won't be experiencing it either, because he doesn't "have" the forgiveness it takes to give away, even though it is and has been available, because God already gave it (Rom 3:24; Col 1:22).

An example of this is from the book *Anne of Green Gables*. In it, Anne accidentally gets Diana Barry drunk. When Diana's mother finds out, Mrs. Barry holds a resentment against Anne. It isn't until Anne saves the life of Mrs. Barry's youngest daughter that Anne is "forgiven" for her earlier mishap. This sounds like

---

7. *MacArthur Study Bible*, 1357.

forgiveness, but in reality it's still just the perform-for-forgiveness trap. True forgiveness must be given as a gift, not earned like a spiritual or relational paycheck.

Remember, "resentment is a relational virus that if not dealt with healthfully spreads from the one we 'hate,' to the ones we love." When I don't forgive others, it's evidence that I am not experiencing His "it is finished" forgiveness (even though it has already been given). God has forgiven me whether I'm living in and experiencing it or not. The problem is that by not accepting Jesus' forgiveness as a free gift, I'll end up attempting to force others to earn their forgiveness from me, in the same way I have been attempting to earn it from Him.

The result: no true forgiveness and continued marital resentments. My not experiencing it, and them not receiving it, is what I and others believe God is talking about in Matthew 6:14–15.

Why do these verses matter in the context of *just love her*? If I don't make a priority of forgiving my "bad" wife, it will eventually result in resentments. But here's one of the other hiccups with resentments. If I don't deal with my resentment healthfully through authentic forgiveness, I will not only blame the person for what they did to me, I will eventually blame my "bad" wife for the resentments I'm holding against her. This is what I call a professional victim. And given enough time and negative self-talk, a relational martyr. We will potentially say, "Not only did you do _____ to me, but your act is so heinous, it's your fault I 'can't' forgive you."

So, why is it so hard for us husbands to forgive and give up our resentments? I believe the answer lies in what I talked about earlier, the idea that "you can't give what you don't have." Again, most Christians are not experiencing true, "it is finished" forgiveness because they don't receive Jesus' forgiveness as a gift, but rather attempt to earn it through worthless good works, or pious self-denial, just like the Jews in Romans (Rom 9:30–33). So, since they "don't have it," they can't, don't, or won't give it. Resentments are held onto because they are not experiencing, and as a by-product not extending, true, gift-form-only forgiveness to their "bad" wives.

Just Love Her

The sins I can't forget are the sins He chooses not to remember. "Oh God, I wanna be like You. You gave me her so that I could be more like You. I want to cherish, love, and forgive, not hold resentments toward her. Thank you!"

One way to get rid of resentments I may have toward my "bad" wife is to remember that the sins I can't forget about her are the sins He chooses not to remember. His grace gives me the ability to love and forgive her in the same way He already loves and forgave the two of us.

1 John 4:12; Hebrews 8:12

But I fear that somehow your pure and undivided devotion to Christ will be corrupted, just as Eve was deceived by the cunning ways of the serpent.

2 Corinthians 11:3

Placing Intellect over Emotion

René Descartes is credited with saying, "I think therefore I am." A more modern rendering might read, "I feel therefore I am." There is this common belief that if I don't feel it or experience it, it's not real, it didn't happen, or it's not who I really am. Again, we place far too much faith in our feelings.

Back in the late '70s, when I first became a Christian, I had a wonderful youth pastor, Greg Carlson, share a helpful train illustration with our youth group. It looked something like this:

The starting point, in this illustration is the engine. It represents thinking on facts or truths from the Bible along with other true-truth resources. Right behind the engine is the coal car. It represents faith or belief along with any accompanying actions and behaviors based on my true-truth thoughts. And finally, the caboose, which represents the emotions or feelings that would be the result or by-product of the actions taken from the facts that were believed in. The goal of this illustration is to try to point out the importance of placing thinking before, above, or over feeling; of developing the discipline of placing our intellect over our emotions, instead of allowing our emotions to override or dictate thinking.

The backward, immature, confused, hurt-filled process of placing emotions over intellect could look something like this:

Greg tried to get us to see the many problems and heartaches that would take place, especially in dating and relational scenarios, if we allowed feelings, emotions, and experiences to cloud and override our thinking.

When you "place too much faith in feelings," adopt the mindset of, "I feel therefore I am," and allow the Feeling's Caboose to get ahead of the Thinking Engine, there's going to be problems. Even as I was looking for these two train illustrations from the Internet, there were a number of sites that were attempting to mess with this time-tested, decision-making sequence by subtitling the illustration, "Let's restore the importance of feelings." I have no problem with feelings. As long as they are in their rightful place. Emotions are wonderful servants, but horrible masters. Great cabooses. Pain-filled engines.

Let's look at this intellect-over-emotion thing a little closer. Bottom line, my emotions are a direct by-product of my predominant thought(s). We kinda covered this earlier. If you want to change your emotion, change your predominant thought. Again, I define predominate as my current or repeated thought. So, let's play a game. If I were to say, "I want you to feel jealous now. Do it now." As I'm telling you to feel jealous, are you feeling jealous? Most likely not.

Let's try something else. If I were to say, "Think of a time in your life when someone you liked either rejected you, disrespected you, or unfavorably compared you to another person." As you bring up a memory of one of these scenarios, if you think about it long enough, there is every likelihood you will feel jealous. Give it a try. Did it work? I'm going to believe it did.

We could do the same thing with happiness or joy. I can say, "Feel happy now." Most likely, you'd say I'm being weird. But if you think of some person, place, position, possession, or thing that makes you happy, or made you happy in the past, and think about it long enough, you will begin to feel happiness or a sense of joy. This is why the Bible says, "Think on these things" (Phil 4:8). What we think about has a huge impact obviously on our thinking and actions but also on our emotions.

Nowhere in the Bible does it say that we are to let our emotions control us. All over the Bible, God tells us to think, meditate, memorize, and consider various truths, doctrines, promises, directives, and attributes of Gods in order to get rid of negative emotions such as anxiety and fear (Josh 1:6–9; Ps 119:9, 11; 1 Cor 10:5). Nowhere in the Bible does it say that we are to marinate or wallow in our emotions (Isa 41:10).

A simple maxim in the context of placing your intellect over emotion is, stop listening to yourself and tell yourself the truth. Just because I think something, doesn't mean it's true. Just because I think something, doesn't mean I have to think it. I can think my way into right emotions and act my way into right emotions. Very simply, if I do something bad I'm gonna feel bad. And most likely, if you do the right thing, you're gonna feel good (Gen 4:3–4).

So, what does this "placing your intellect over your emotion" have to do with our "bad" marriages? Everything! When the disciples were in the boat and their predominant thoughts were on the wind and the unruly waves, their emotions were completely out of control and full of panic. When they finally remembered that Jesus was in the back of the boat and focused on Him, their predominant thoughts changed, as did their emotions of panic and fear. Especially after He calmed the storm (Matt 8:23–28).

Another example of this was when Joshua had to take over for one of the greatest leaders of all time, Moses. This was a tough act to follow. God, understanding what Joshua would be facing, told him, "No one will be able to stand against you as long as you live. For I will be with you as I was with Moses. I will not fail you or abandon you" (Josh 1:5). God then went on to tell Joshua to keep his predominant thoughts focused on Him and what He had promised. In 1:7 God told Joshua to "be strong and very courageous. Be careful to obey all the instructions Moses gave you. Do not deviate from them, turning either to the right or to the left. Then you will be successful in everything you do." God was telling Joshua to place his intellect over his emotions by keeping his eyes on God (predominant thoughts) and believe in His promises and directives, not potential failures or inadequacies (1:8–9).

We're going to have to do the same thing in our "bad" marriages. We're going to have to place our intellect over our emotion and make our predominant thoughts of how Jesus is our number one love and will never leave us or forsake us (Heb 13:5–6), and that He has a "good" plan for our "bad" marriages (Jer 29:11).

If you want more help with this placing your intellect over emotions thing, consider reading *Spiritual Depression*, by Martyn Lloyd-Jones, or *Telling Yourself the Truth*, by Dr. William Backus and Marie Chapian. Both of these wonderful books helped me see more clearly what Greg was trying to teach us all those years ago: the simple yet powerful truth of placing your intellect over your emotion.

Instead of the constant focus on sex (or the lack of it), or butts, boobs, and hairdos, acknowledge that she has shown a fear of God by just sticking with you.

Proverbs 31:30

"I Choose Us"

My wife and I watched a movie years ago where the wife in the movie had a cute little phrase she liked to say to her husband that went something like, "I choose us." I really like that! But I'm gonna fiddle with it a little bit. I want to suggest that the first "I choose us" is directed toward our number one love, Jesus: our second, toward our "bad" wives. One of the first places to start in your desire to glorify God and *just love her* in your "bad" marriage will be to pray that He would be your number one love and she would be your second. It will be impossible to have any of the information from this little book work until He helps you authentically say, "I choose *us*."

Even though I'm confused about where the two of us are in our "bad" marriage, and confused about where it's headed, and even if it never changes, I choose to embrace it, because even though how it's going isn't my first choice, I know it's *Yours*.

Mark 10:9; 1 Corinthians 13:7

You Are My Life; She Is My Wife

This phrase is a wonderful little reminder of Mark 12:30. The problem with this reminder, especially if you perceive yourself as having a "bad" wife and a "bad" marriage, is that you've probably got this one backwards. You might not say it out loud, but the dissatisfaction, lack of fulfillment, and chaos in your marriage may be a by-product of your internally saying, "She is my life, You are my just-in-case." Spaced repetition of a worthy ideal, idea, or Bible verse (Ps 119:9, 11) creates a passion. God can use this little phrase to straighten out my reversed passions. You are my life. She is my wife.

Is there a possibility that Jesus put the two of you together in your "bad" marriage so that His power could be "displayed and illustrated" to a world that can't do marriage without Him? "While He was passing by, He noticed a man [who had been] blind from birth . . . Jesus answered, he was born so that the works of God might be displayed and illustrated in him."

John 9:1–3

A Full Life

I'm sure you figured this out by now, but if you're struggling in your marriage, the rest of your life stinks. You can be at work, play, exercise, shopping, whatever, but if your wife and you are struggling, your glass of life is half full (at best). One of the reasons for writing this little book, is taken from John 10:10 where Jesus said, "I have come that they may have life and have it to the full." I'm going to believe that when Jesus said this, the first "fullnesser" He was referring to was Himself; the second, our marriages.

You wanna love her more? Daily remind yourself of how He forgave all your sin.

"But one who is forgiven little, shows little love."

Luke 7:47

Taking What Matters into My Own Hands

There's this comforting and powerful verse in Revelation 3:7 that says, "What He opens no one can shut, and what He shuts no one can open." Isn't it interesting that when we first met our "bad" wife, we were unbelievably grateful to God, who "opened that relational door?" Now after x number of years, and actually getting to know rather than just fantasize about her, we're wanting to close the relational door that God opened.

Martin Luther had this amazingly painful quote which said, "The sin underneath all our sins is to trust the lie of the serpent that we cannot trust the love and grace of Christ and must take matters into our own hands."[8]

How true is that? God opened the door to your "bad" marriage, but due to various relational sufferings and disappointments you now want to shut it. Due to various relational sufferings and the perceived "badnesses" of your marriage, you stopped "trusting the love and grace of Christ" for yourself and your "bad" wife.

Your best efforts got you here. Where you're at right now in your relationship is because you attempted to take control through your plans and your efforts. Let it go. Whatever it is that you have taken into your own hands, let it go. He can handle it better than you.

---

8. Taken from https://www.goodreads.com/quotes/tag/god-s-love.

Whenever I place His will above mine in my "bad" marriage, He gets glorified.

John 13:31–32; John 15:5; Galatians 2:20

Primarily Sacrifice and Courage

We want to make it all about emotions. Broken people always look for immediate emotional gratification. Delayed gratification, work, long-term sacrifice are qualities that are not on the relational radar screen of dissatisfied, "empty," needy people. But here's a thought, in what most church people would call the "love chapter" (1 Cor 13), feelings and/or emotions are not listed as one of the characteristics of love. Sacrifice and courage are.

The second you start nitpicking, pointing out faults, or feeling sorry for yourself—worship!

Habakkuk 3:17–19

Let's Talk about Sex

Well, this is a big and scary topic. I'm not going to try to cover everything in this area, possibly for my own safety, and most likely because I wouldn't know what I'm talking about. But here's just a few thoughts that come to mind.

Sex as the main course in a marriage is the equivalence of a TwinkieBurger. It looks and sounds like fun, but like high fructose sugars, it doesn't last. There's an immediate high, with an accompanying low. Sex ain't meat and potatoes. At best it's the cherry on top of the sacrifice and courage you've been serving up in your marriage on a daily basis.

This next point is pretty important and might help explain why you are struggling in your sex life (if you are). Proverbs 9:17 says, "Stolen water is sweet; food eaten in secret is delicious!" In other words, when you do something you're not supposed to do, there's always an added titillation that goes along with the activity. The Bible says no sex before marriage (1 Cor 6:18, 7:2; Heb 13:4). So, if you had sex before marriage, it was obviously exciting, or you wouldn't have "broken the law" and gone against what God said you weren't supposed to do. Sex as a Christian is "legal" within marriage. The problem now that you're married is that you don't have the added titillation of "drinking stolen water." In marriage, what used to be so "sweet" no longer is. You took the "stolenness" out of your sex life. He can renew your legit sex life. Just ask.

Next point. Ephesians 5:22 says, "You wives must submit to your husbands' leadership . . ." Just a thought here, if you and your wife didn't respect God's authority when He said no to sex before marriage, she won't respect His and your authority when you ask to have sex after marriage (1 Cor 7:5). She most likely won't even know what's going on, but because she hasn't learned or developed the Spirit-inspired character trait of submission to authority, sex may be a problem in your "bad" marriage (1 Pet 3:6).

Next point. Friendship is rare, sex is common. Friendships that blossom into married-sex relationships are rare. Premarital sex relationships that stumble into sexless marriages are common.

If you did have sex before marriage, there's every likelihood sex or sex-like stuff has become an idol to you. Remember, an idol is that thing I run to in order to get significant needs met instead of running to Jesus. In the context of sex-idol stuff, when God says no, and you say yes, eventually it's going to bite you (Rom 6:16). If you keep saying yes long enough, when you should have said no, sex becomes an accepted and many times unidentified idol. Many times this unidentified idol remains unidentified until you get married and find out your unrealistic expectation of being able to experience your sex idol whenever you want, just ain't gonna happen, and is most likely even now causing serious problems.

The next piece that might be important to look at is to find a new passion for your wife other than sex. This is important to consider because God is eventually going to take away your sex-idol stuff (Exod 20:3). So, in the context of the weaning or possibly ripping away of your sex-idol, you might want to ask Him to help you find a new passion for your wife other than sex.

Side note: I'm really grateful that my wife and I didn't have sex before we got married. Thank you, Jesus! I messed up in this area long before I started dating my wife, and the pain of that experience made me wise enough to stay away from repeating it. Even though Laurie and I didn't have sex while dating, I already had my sex-idol in place.

For the past almost thirty-ish years, God has been ripping away my sex-idol stuff. The problem is, the ripping away really, really hurts. One of the new passions God has given me for my wife, who is not a "dripping faucet," not chaotic, not a whiner or complainer, is that she continues to love me, after all these years, even when I don't deserve it. Whenever I call and I hear, "Hi, honey," all my relational stars align, and life is good. Another new passion

Just Love Her

God has given me for my wife is the fact that for over twenty years now, Laurie has been tirelessly taking care of our son Sammy and has never once complained. Talk about your Proverbs 31 wife! Yep! Priceless new passion!

Just a reminder, Mach 3 with your hair on fire is far less important than peace, calm, no chaos, and no "dripping faucets" (Prov 27:15–16).

Just a thought: Proverbs 31 has always been the ultimate-Christian-wife chapter in the Bible. Isn't it interesting that when the wisest man in the world (besides Jesus—Matt 12:42), gives the characteristics of a wife of noble character, he never mentions anything about emotions or sex?

Overall, in order to either undo or do any of this stuff involved with your sex-idol stuff, I encourage you to ask God on a daily basis that He be your number one passion and love. It will be impossible to do away with your sex-idol stuff without this new passion for Him and the help of the Holy Spirit. Warning: this process of Him making Himself your number one passion is really, really painful. Painful, but worth it.

In regard to loneliness, there's a difference between solitude and isolation. Solitude is a loving response to a spiritual invitation; isolation, an unhealthy retreat. One results in intimacy with Jesus, the other, loneliness.

Psalm 27:8

Which Is a Bigger Deal?

Which is a bigger deal, the fact that I can never be separated from His love or that I feel separated from hers?

Romans 8:39 says that "nothing will ever separate us from the love of God." Proverbs 24:18 says, "He's a friend that sticks closer than a brother." Hebrews 13:5 says, "Never will I leave you; never will I forsake you." Romans 8:9–11 and John 14:16 both say that we have the Holy Spirit living inside of us. The simple reality is, we're never alone. We're never without Him. No one could ever be closer, no one could ever be less separated from us than Jesus.

I hear people pray things like, "Oh God, please draw near," or the title to the old Maranatha Praise Band song, "Make Your Presence Known." The problem with these two and many other requests is, He already has. Like the verses I just listed, and many others, He's already drawn near and made His presence known. We get in trouble because we trust our feelings more than we trust who God is and what the Bible says about how He relates to us.

When we don't trust Him and what the Bible says about His love for us and how He expresses that love toward us, we're gonna end up looking for some person to do what only God can and has already done toward and for us. But when we do this, she, most likely our "bad" wife, will eventually be unable to do what God has already done and we'll end up feeling separated from Him and her.

Here's a couple of thoughts on how to improve our awareness of the God who is already Immanuel ("God with us"). The first is to use our biblically based, worship-oriented, sanctified imagination to "experience" God. An example of this could be found in Psalm 73. Verse 23 says, ". . . yet I still belong to You." These words excite and move me. When I look at how sinful, idolatrous, self-centered, and rebellious I am, and He still chooses to love, forgive, and accept me, I break down, and at times with internal tears along with David say, "I still belong to You." Thank you, Abba! Amazing!

My Psalm 73, sanctified-imagination thing looks something like this. I picture Jesus as the captain of the Saturday morning grade school dodgeball team. Even though I'm the worst player out there, He chooses me first. I don't deserve to be chosen. I can't catch or throw the ball. But even with my obvious weaknesses, inabilities, and past failures, He chose me! I've never been chosen first for anything in my life! But now I'm on His team! I belong!

Another way to experience God is to use the five love languages developed by Gary Chapman. The five love languages include: words of affirmation, quality time, receiving gifts, acts of service, and physical touch. You're gonna have to use your sanctified imagination in this exercise, as well, but I think this really works.

The first thing to do is either get the book or jump online and figure out what your love language is. Next, apply your love language(s) to Jesus. An example of this would be to consider my love language, which is acts of kindness. What I can do, during my time with Jesus while reading the Bible, is to make a priority of looking for the acts of kindness Jesus has already done for me. The obvious and most important act He did for me was to die on the cross and give me spiritual life. I was spiritually dead, hopeless, helpless, alone, and on my way to hell. Jesus' act of kindness of dying on the cross for me gets me excited. Even as I'm writing this, I'm semi-emotional and unbelievably grateful for His act of kindness for me. I didn't deserve it. But He acted for me. This helps me more deeply experience His love for me that was already there before time ever was (Eph 1:4).

Another way to experience my relationship with Jesus is to doctrine myself into love with Him. Use the amazing doctrines from the Bible as a relational Hallmark card to help experience Jesus' love. An example of this would be to look at the primary doctrine of justification by faith (Rom 3:27–28; 5:18–19; 10:9–11). This doctrine acknowledges that I am a helpless, hopeless, rebellious sinner on my way to hell, and yet Jesus declares me justified; just like I'd always obeyed. I'm emotionally, spiritually, psychologically, relationally, and maritally marinating in my relational screwups and yet God chooses to look at me as if I'd always obeyed! Oh my goodness! Even as I'm writing this right now, I think, "I love You, Jesus! Thank You so much for loving and forgiving me even when I'm such a screwup!"

So, to answer the above question, which is a bigger deal; obviously it's that we will never be separated from Jesus' love. The reason we don't make a big deal of this is because we place too much faith in our feelings and not enough faith in the factual truths of the Bible. If and when I rest in God's amazing love and acceptance toward me (that is already there and will never not be there), the little hiccups I'm experiencing with my "bad" wife that make me feel separated from Him and her seem to fade as I realize that I can never be separated from Him (Rom 8:31–39).

Jesus never tells us to do anything that He hasn't already done to and for us. I wonder if I understood that Jesus loves me with all His heart, all His soul, and all His mind, that this reality might make it easier to love her as much as I have already been loved by Him?

Matthew 22:37–40

The Exchanged Life

I think the first time I was exposed to Major Ian Thomas and his thoughts on "the exchanged life" was through my mother and the major's book, entitled *The Saving Life of Christ*. I remember seeing it lying next to her Bible in her study way back when I was a freshman in high school. I wasn't a Christian at the time, but I remember the title and even more, I remember my mom's life. My mom lived the exchanged life.

The next time I was exposed to Major Thomas and his exchanged life principles was during my first year at Bible college. He was one of the first speakers during chapel that year and he completely blew me away. He said things like, "I can't. You never said I could. You can. You always said you would." Or, "We vacate, He occupies."[9] He used verses like Romans 5:10, which says, "Much more than having been saved by His death we shall be saved by His life." Or Galatians 2:20, "I have been crucified with Christ and it is no longer I who live but Christ lives in me and the life which I now live in the flesh, I live by faith in the son of God who loved me and delivered Himself up for me."

These verses and sayings are all about me getting out of the way and letting God get back in. The exchanged life is not a life of my inactivity but one of miraculous "Him-activity" through me. He does the work. He just does it. He jumps into the needed, impossible-on-my-own activity and supernaturally gets it done. That's the exchanged life.

It's seen in Isaiah 30:15, which says, "In quietness and trust is your strength." Or Colossians 1:10 where Paul says, "I labor according to His mighty power that works within me." This is the

---

9. Thomas, *Saving Life*, class notes.

exchanged life and it's what's needed in order to *just love her* the way God already loves her. We're going to have to, with God's help, get out of the way and let Him live His life in and through us in our "bad" marriages.

I have two choices. I can either blame or change.

Colossians 3:12–14

The First Evidence of Change

I think this next little thought is fairly important. Most everyone wants to change. Most likely that's the reason you're reading this little book. The problem with change is, if and when it happens, it takes a really long time. Because it takes so long, and because much of the time we're looking for the wrong evidences of change, we quit.

The good news is that God never does. Philippians 1:6 says, "And I am certain that God, who began the good work within you, will continue His work until it is finally finished on the day when Christ Jesus returns." Hebrews 11:1 says, "Faith shows the reality of what we hope for; it is the evidence of things we cannot see." The first evidence of change is that He said He's going to change us.

Jesus, I choose to glorify You in the middle of my "bad" marriage.

Hebrews 12:2

If It's Worth Doing It's Worth Doing Badly

I once heard someone say something like, "If it's worth doing it's worth doing badly." This is a short, simple, self-talk thought that can be used to keep you going instead of quitting.

A goofy but simple illustration of this would be when my mother was attempting to teach my dyslexic brain how to tie my shoes. Her teaching technique of choice was the little shoelace bunny rabbit. This method used an imaginary bunny that magically jumped in, around, and through holes made from my shoelaces.

It didn't make sense to me then and it still doesn't. My point is that I didn't give up. When I first started tying my shoes I did it badly. I continued to do it badly (I don't think they invented Velcro yet), because it was worth doing and needed to get done. This morning the little shoelace bunny did his thing with really no effort on my part (still no Velcro). After all these years I no longer do it badly because I didn't quit.

The same is true of our "bad" marriages. Since it's worth doing, keep doing it. Even if you're doing it badly, don't quit! Before any more "doing it badly," ask Jesus to be your number one passion. Next, gab the Bible and Ian Thomas's *The Saving Life of Christ* and ask God to live His exchanged life through you in your "bad" marriage (Gal 2:20). Don't give up! And eventually and hopefully, you won't do it badly.

Get rid of all relational memorabilia.

Genesis 19:26

The Number One Indicator of Success in Life

It's not about what was or wasn't named after you, not the house you live in or the car you drive. It's not the schools you went to or the degrees you got. It's not the size of your bank account or waist. The number one indicator of success in life is measured by how you do relationships.

"'You must love the Lord your God with all your heart, all your soul, all your mind, and all your strength.' The second [commandment] is equally important: 'Love your neighbor as yourself.' No other commandment is greater than these" (Mark 12:30–31).

Given enough time and God-provided surrender, pain and suffering become a tender reminder of His presence in my life. "We continue to shout our praise even when we're hemmed in with troubles, because we know how troubles can develop passionate patience in us, and how that patience in turn forges the tempered steel of virtue, keeping us alert for whatever God will do next. In alert expectancy such as this, we're never left feeling shortchanged. Quite the contrary—we can't round up enough containers to hold everything God generously pours into our lives through the Holy Spirit!"

Romans 5:3–5

Jesus Loved Judas

Here's an interesting thought. In the Gospels, when Jesus said, "*One of you guys is going to betray me,*" all twelve of them looked around and asked, "Is it me?" Jesus obviously knew in advance that Judas was going to betray Him. He also knew that Satan had already possessed Judas (Luke 22:3), yet even with this reality, Jesus washed Judas' feet (John 13:1–17). Jesus loved Judas in such a way that none of the other eleven knew that he was the betrayer. If Jesus could love the one who sold Him out for thirty pieces of silver and arranged His murder, maybe we, in and through His power, can supernaturally love our "bad" wives?

I wonder if the primary reason our marriages turned "bad" was because we took our eyes off Him and focused on her?

John 13:29–30

Take What You've Been Given and Pass It On

You can't give what you don't have, not even to yourself, let alone to your "bad" wife. The Bible, in 1 John 4:10, says that we've been given something pretty special. It reads, "This is real love—not that we loved God, but that He loved us and sent His Son as a sacrifice to take away our sins." So, what if you focus on the fact that He's the initiator and the perpetuator of this supernatural love toward you, and you, in return, pass that supernatural love, in His power, on to your "bad" wife?

Infatuaters, twitterpaters, and idolaters: "Take this rule: whatever weakens your reason, impairs the tenderness of your conscience, obscures your sense of God, or takes off your relish of spiritual things; in short, whatever increases the strength and authority of your body over your mind; that thing is sin to you, however innocent it may be in itself."[10]

Susanna Wesley, June 8, 1725

10. From a letter to her son, John Wesley (*Susanna Wesley*, 109).

Pick Up Your Cross Daily and Follow Me

In Luke 9:23, Jesus says, "Whoever wants to be My disciple must deny themselves and take up their cross daily and follow Me." What if one of the evidences of our being Jesus' disciple was to deny ourselves (be less selfish and self-centered), pick up our marital "cross" daily, and make a bigger deal of following Him, than that our "bad" wife isn't following us and our plan for our "bad" marriage?

Try not to confuse the pain, loss, and sufferings of your "bad" marriage with lack of love, abandonment, or punishments from Him for our previous sins.

Proverbs 3:11–12

Stick It Out!

You know, the crazy, lovesick, running around at night, looking for her husband "young woman" from the Song of Solomon? That "young woman" who says, "Kiss me and kiss me again, for your love is sweeter than wine" (Song 1:2–4)? What if God didn't give you her? What if God gave you a Gomer (Hos 1:2), a Michal (2 Sam 6:20–23), or a Delilah (Judg 16)? Obviously you didn't get one of them either, but, is there a possibility that in your mind, God gave you someone worse, your "bad" wife?

Even if, in your mind, you think you got the relational short end of the stick, the Bible says to stick it out (Mal 2:16; Matt 5:32). First Corinthians 7:17 says, "And don't be wishing you were someplace else or with someone else. Where you are right now is God's place for you. Live and obey and love and believe right there. God, not your marital status, defines your life. Don't think I'm being harder on you than on the others. I give this same counsel in all the churches" (*The Message*).

The general principle when the "what-ifs" of marriage start turning up is to stay put. Stay together. The overall emphasis of 1 Corinthians 7 is to stick it out! The primary emphasis is not my happiness, satisfaction, and/or fulfillment, but God's. God has different priorities for your "bad" marriage than you do. Just because my "bad" marriage is less than perfect, doesn't mean I get to bail (1 Pet 2:19).

The story is told of a Christian lawyer who was talking to a Christian husband contemplating divorce who said, "About the only people who profit from divorces are the attorneys!"

Stick it out!

When the panic attacks, confusions, depressions, and despair hit, remember, the wind and the waves remembered His voice.
Ask God to give you that same ability.
"When Jesus woke up, He rebuked the wind and said to the waves, 'Silence! Be still!'" Suddenly the wind stopped, and there was a great calm."

Mark 4:39; Genesis 1:1–2

The Christian-Marriage Martyr

It was kind of stupid and pretty judgmental, but the guys in my freshman dorm during my first year at Bible college sat around and made up this unspoken (outside of our dorm room) hierarchy of which students were spiritual and which ones weren't. It was this kind of imaginary ladder that ranked student's spirituality. It looked something like this: The lowest rung was reserved for those girls who weren't going for a specific program, but just "auditing" classes with the hope of snatching a Christian husband and taking him back to the farm in Kansas. The next rung up was for music directors; next, youth pastors; then head pastors; and finally the big kahuna, the highest rung of spiritual coolness was reserved for overseas missionaries.

It's been over forty years since those undergraduate days. Since then, I'm pretty sure I unconsciously added another rung. I'm not saying this is right or accurate and probably shouldn't be said out loud, but I have since placed those who have been or will be martyred for their faith in Jesus at the top of this imaginary ladder (Rev 20:4–6 *The Message*).

Ephesians 5 is the big kahuna of chapters in the Bible of how husbands are supposed to treat their wives (Eph 5:21–33). These verses tell us husbands that we're supposed to give our lives for our wives in the same way Jesus gave His life for His church. The love we are to give to our wives is exemplified for us when Jesus gave His life for His church in vv. 25 and 28. I wonder if this is an example for us husbands of being a Christian-marriage martyr?

James and Marti Hefley, in their book *By Their Blood: Christian Martyrs from the Twentieth Century and Beyond*, identify a martyr as "one who dies, suffers or sacrifices everything for a principal...[11]"

I wonder if this could apply to our "whom God has put together" "bad" marriages? Is there a possibility that remaining in the suffering and continuing to sacrifice for the "principle" of glorifying God in the middle of our "bad" marriages could be a form of Christian-marriage martyrdom?

---

11. Hefley and Hefley, *By Their Blood*, 9.

In the middle of the loneliness, ask Jesus to help you remember and experience Him inside of you.

John 14:27–29

It's Not Good for Guys to Be Alone

It's really sad when a volleyball ends up being your best friend. It's even worse when you emotionally lose it when your BFF, Wilson the ball, rolls overboard. If you've seen the movie *Castaway*, with Tom Hanks, you'll recognize this scene and a number of pretty realistic pictures of the downside of loneliness.

I didn't get married until I was in my early forties. Friday nights without a date really stunk. But worse than my dateless nights as a single person was being alone every night while divorced for seven years. It's one thing to be alone because you haven't found the "right one." It's another thing to be alone because you lost the "right one." It's not good for guys to be alone. Maybe your "bad" marriage is better than crying over lost volleyballs?

The adulterer and the idolator struggle with the same sin, only at polar opposites of the martial continuum.

Revelation 2:14

Maybe She's God's Tool?

What if the major problems you're having in your "bad" marriage are actually areas of idolatry that God is using your "bad" wife as His tool to wean you away from? What if she's God's tool to help you focus on and not be distracted away from your number one passion, Jesus? Maybe she's God's tool?

I wonder if after your love relationship with Jesus, she might be your dearest earthly treasure?

Matthew 13:44–46

Annoyances Are My Problem Not Hers

You've heard the old adage that we're not supposed to "make mountains out of mole hills." Annoyances are nothing more than relational molehills. If she's not doing anything illegal, immoral, or unhealthy, that's an annoyance and it's my problem not hers. Annoyances are little more than relational dung piles. The goal with dung piles is to walk around, not through them. Isn't it interesting that the majority of relational discord, distance, and divorce are usually caused, at least initially, by annoying molehills not mountains? Annoyances are my problem, not hers.

Wouldn't it be neat if we could do that 1 Corinthians 13 thing of "not taking into account a wrong suffered" and realize that annoyances are my problem, not hers?

1 Corinthians 13:5

Provide. Protect. Be Present.
The 3P's of Just Loving Her.

Have Fun. Be Faithful. Be Friends.
The 3F's of Just Loving Her.

She's the Biggest Mistake of My Life

Have you said or thought it yet? "She's the biggest mistake of my life." Goofy thoughts like this are divorces waiting to happen. We have a tendency to think that what I think is no big deal as long as I don't say it out loud or act on it. We think that because nobody can see or hear what we're thinking, there's no danger. The problem with thinking like that is that it's completely wrong. Given enough time, the right circumstances, the junk you've allowed to roll around in your noggin, with no seemingly negative repercussions, will eventually be the verbal (hopefully not physical) ammunition we use during our next argument that seriously wounds our "bad" wives (Phil 4:8).

I wonder if the "drawn" in this verse looks more like the wayward sheep, with the broken leg on the shoulder of the loving shepherd, than a Hallmark card? Could God be "drawing" you to Himself through your "bad" marriage?

"I have loved you, My people, with an everlasting love. With unfailing love I have drawn you to Myself."

Jeremiah 31:3

God loves your "bad" wife as much as He loves Jesus.

John 17:23

I wonder if the majority of Christians are not experiencing the forgiveness that is already theirs?

Romans 9:30–33

Why is this a big deal? You can't give as a free gift something you're attempting to earn by performance.
This includes your "bad" wife.

If I'm more concerned with her sin, not mine, I have a serious problem in my relationship with Jesus.

Luke 7:47–48

Fewer expectations and more acceptance. Less pointing out perceived faults and more prayer.

Proverbs 11:12; Matthew 7:3

God would never tell us to do anything He hasn't already done to and for us. Forgive her!

Matthew 18:22

When I sin, I'm cheating God's plan and process for growth in my life. The result will be immediate gratification with an aftertaste of confusion, fear, and loneliness.

Genesis 3:8

Since You are glorified through the death and sufferings of Your Son and Christian martyrs, why not my "bad" marriage.

John 13:31

Conclusion

WELL, THAT'S IT! I sincerely hope you found something in this little book that will restore your intimate love affair with and number one passion for Jesus. Like I said in the preface, the core; the center; the hub; the apex, everything in the Christian life revolves around Jesus. "I can do all things through Him who strengthens me," and "apart from Him I can do nothing" (Phil 4:13; John 15:5). This obviously includes doing our "bad"-marriage thing.

The key to the Christian life is to keep Him the center of life. Remembering that He is your life, she is your wife. He is your soulmate. She is your "helpmate." There is no true joy in life unless He is your true joy. He has to be your number one preoccupation, concern, and object of worship. The key to having a good, not "bad," marriage is your relationship with Jesus. If He were your number one passion, she wouldn't be your number one problem.

Please know and remember that His plan for your life is far better than your plan for your life. Psalm 138:8 says, "The Lord will work out His plans for my life." Whatever your plan was, it got you here and in your "bad" marriage. If you hang onto your plan, you'll miss His plan for your life (Matt 16:25; John 10:10).

The path to a good and not "bad" marriage is a backdoor approach. That path goes through your intimate love relationship with Jesus (Prov 16:7). As He takes away your relational idols and places Himself in His rightful, number one relational slot, your relationship with your wife has a much better chance of improving. She no longer needs to be your number one need-meeter because Jesus has reclaimed that position and you can now leave her alone.

Now glory be to God, who by His mighty power at work within us is able to do far more in our *"bad" marriages* than we would ever dare to ask or even dream of—infinitely beyond our highest prayers, desires, thoughts, or hopes. May He be given glory forever and ever through endless ages because of His master plan for our *"whom God has put together, let no one separate" marriage* through Jesus Christ. (Paraphrase of Eph 3:20–21 Living Bible)

Bibliography

Backus, William, and Marie Chapian. *Telling Yourself the Truth*. Minneapolis: Bethany Fellowship, 1980.

Bridges, Jerry. *Trusting God*. Colorado Springs: NavPress, 1988.

Fitzpatrick, Elyse. *Because He Loves Me*. Wheaton, IL: Crossway, 2008.

Flavel, John. *Triumphing over Sinful Fear*. Edited by J. Stephen Yuille. Grand Rapids: Reformation Heritage, 2011.

Foxe, John. *Foxe's Book of Martyrs: Abridged from Milner's Edition*. London: Routledge, 1851.

Hefley, James, and Marti Hefley. *By Their Blood: Christian Martyrs from the Twentieth Century and Beyond*. Road Ada, MI: Baker, 2004.

Hurnard, Hannah. *Hinds' Feet on High Places*. London: Olive, 1951.

Keller, Timothy. *Counterfeit Gods : When the Empty Promises of Love, Money and Power Let You Down*. London : Hodder & Stoughton, 2009.

Keller, Timothy, and Kathy Keller. *The Meaning of Marriage: Facing the Complexities of Commitment with the Wisdom of God*. New York: Viking, 2011.

Kittel, Gerhard Friedrich, ed. *Theological Dictionary of the New Testament*. Grand Rapids: Eerdmans, 1992.

Lloyd-Jones, Martyn. *Spiritual Depression*. London: Pickering & Inglis, 1965.

MacArthur, John, ed. *The MacArthur Study Bible*. Updated ed. La Habra, CA: Nelson, 1995.

Packer, J. I. *Knowing God*. Downers Grove: InterVarsity, 1973.

Piper, John. *Desiring God*. Leicester, UK: InterVarsity, 1986.

Thomas, W. Ian. *The Saving Life of Christ*. Estes Park, CO: Torchbearers, 1961.

Wesley, Susanna. *Susanna Wesley: The Complete Writings*. Edited by Charles Wallace Jr. Oxford: Oxford University Press, 1997.

Wilson, Sandra. *Hurt People Hurt People: Hope and Healing for Yourself and Your Relationships*. Grand Rapids: Our Daily Bread, 2015.

www.ingramcontent.com/pod-product-compliance
Lightning Source LLC
Chambersburg PA
CBHW050147170426
43197CB00011B/1990